The Truth about Mary

The Truth about Mary

A Theological and Philosophical Evaluation of the Proposed Fifth Marian Dogma

PETER S. DILLARD

WIPF & STOCK · Eugene, Oregon

THE TRUTH ABOUT MARY
A Theological and Philosophical Evaluation of the Proposed Fifth
Marian Dogma

Wipf & Stock
A Division of Wipf and Stock Publishers
199 W. 8th Ave., Suite 3
Eugene, OR 97401

www.wipfandstock.com

ISBN 13: 978-1-60608-226-3

Manufactured in the U.S.A.

For my mother,
who taught me about our Mother
without even knowing it

Mary Immaculate
Merely a woman, yet
Whose presence, power is
Great as no goddess's
Was deemèd, dreamèd; who
This one work has to do—
Let all God's glory through,
God's glory which would go
Through her and from her flow
Off, and no way but so.

Gerard Manley Hopkins
*The Blessed Virgin compared to
the Air we Breathe*

Contents

Introduction

THE CHURCH teaches at least three dogmas regarding the Blessed Virgin Mary: her Divine Motherhood (*Theotokos*), her Perpetual Virginity, her Immaculate Conception, and her Assumption into Heaven.[1] In recent years, a popular movement known as Vox Populi Mariae Mediatrici, or Voice of the People for Mary Mediatrix, has arisen in support of a papal definition of a fifth Marian dogma declaring that Mary is Co-Redemptrix, Mediatrix of all graces, and Advocate.[2] The Vox Populi movement

---

1. The three definite dogmas were declared, respectively, by the Council of Ephesus in 431, the Second Council of Constantinople in 553, Pope Pius IX in 1854, and Pope Pius XII in 1950. Though many regard the description of Mary as *aeiparthenos*, or ever virgin, by the Second Council of Constantinople in 553 as a dogma, it might be objected that there is no clear evidence that the Council intended to define Mary's Perpetual Virginity as a dogma, or even as a definitive teaching. A possible reply is that the proposition that Mary is ever virgin, even if not a solemnly defined dogma in the strict sense, is nonetheless a formally revealed truth implicit in the deposit of faith that has become explicit in the fullness of time, as evidenced not only by the crystalization of Patristic formulas such as "A virgin conceived, a virgin gave birth, and a virgin remained (St. Augustine) but, more importantly, by centuries of the faithful continuing to address Mary as "Blessed Virgin" even though she now dwells in Heaven. However, for our purpose here it is not necessary to resolve this dispute. The question before us is whether the formal definition of a dogma proclaiming Mary to be Co-Redemptrix, Mediatrix of all graces, and Advocate is currently warranted, not whether there are three or four previous Marian dogmas. As a matter of convenience I will continue to speak of "the proposed fifth Marian dogma."

2. The Vox Populi Mariae Mediatrici website can be found at www.voxpopuli.org.

has effectively utilized the Internet to extend the boundaries of traditional theological discourse in an original and provocative manner.[3]

There has also been significant opposition to the definition of a fifth Marian dogma. The Twelfth International Mariological Conference held in Czestochowa, Poland in August 1996 enumerated various theological and ecumenical concerns about the proposed dogma.[4] Some of these concerns are echoed in a published statement by the staff of *Marianum*, a premier journal of Mariology.[5] Proponents of the proposed dogma have responded to these objections.[6] Thus the controversy continues unabated.

The proposed dogma consists of three claims:

(C1) Mary is Co-Redemptrix because she cooperates preeminently with Christ in the work of redemption.

(C2) Mary is Mediatrix of all graces because she mediates any and all graces merited by Christ which are bestowed upon us.

(C3) Mary is Advocate because she acts as our principle intercessor before Christ.

---

3. Another website actively engaged in promoting the definition of a fifth Marian dogma is www.airmaria.com. See particularly the video episodes of "MaryCast" and "Co-Redemptrix, Mediatrix, Advocate" presented by Dr. Mark Miravalle.

4. The results of the Czestochowa Congress are published in "Declaration of the Theological Commission of the Pontifical Marian Academy," *L'Osservatore Romano* (June 4, 1997).

5. In *The Marian Library Newsletter* No.38 (New Series) Summer 1999, available online at http://campus.udayton.edu/mary/respub/summer99.html#3.

6. For example, Dr. Mark Miravalle, "In Continued Dialogue with the Czestochowa Commission," presented at the International Symposium on Marian Co-redemption, "*Maria Mater Unitatis*, held at Downside Abbey, Stratton-on-the-Fosse, England on August 24, 2002. Miravalle's paper can be found online at www.voxpopuli.org/czestochowa.pdf.

Concerning each of these claims, a number of questions can be raised. What, if any, are the Scriptural foundations for the claim? What is the history of the Church's teachings regarding the claim? What, if any, is the theological basis for the claim? How might the claim be clarified philosophically?

In this study I shall mostly confine myself to the theological and philosophical questions about the three claims which constitute the proposed fifth Marian dogma, appealing to Scriptural and ecclesiastical considerations only when they are directly relevant. Let me explain why I restrict my inquiry in this way, how I propose to answer the theological and philosophical questions about the three constituent claims, and what my answers to these questions will be.

Why do I confine myself to theological and philosophical questions about the claims that Mary is Co-Redemptrix, Mediatrix of all graces, and Advocate? My principle justification begins with the observation that the issue of whether the proposed fifth Marian dogma should be formally defined by the magisterium remains unresolved in the Church today.[7] There are people of good faith on both sides. Part of the reason the issue remains unresolved is that, as we shall see, each of the claims in question may be interpreted as making a number of different assertions. Disambiguation of the claims is thus essential before any formal definition is in order; otherwise, the Church is being asked to proclaim an ambiguity as a dogma, which can only foster confusion among the faithful. Even after the multiple senses of one of the controversial claims have been clearly identified, no formal definition which includes the claim is in order until

7. A formal definition by the extraordinary magisterium would issue either from the pope speaking ex cathedra or from the bishops in union with the pope defining doctrine at an ecumenical council. A doctrine definitively taught by the ordinary universal magisterium consisting of the bishops, though dispersed, in unity and unison would also become a dogma. Most proponents of the fifth Marian dogma seek a papal definition.

a convincing case has been made that the claim, interpreted in at least one of these senses, is a proper object of infallibility, and that the claim is not repugnant to human reason. In the process of disambiguation, doctrinal development, and elucidation, the tools of theological and philosophical analysis are no less indispensable than Scriptural exegesis and ecclesiastical review.

How should we try to answer theological and philosophical questions about the three claims which make up the proposed dogma? Here we confront the matter of methodology. Since theology and philosophy are distinct disciplines, in each case my approach will be somewhat different. For a proposition to a proper object of infallibility—more precisely, the proper object of a formal definition infallibly declared by the extraordinary magisterium or definitively taught by the ordinary and universal magisterium—the proposition must be shown to be either a formally revealed truth or something that, although not itself formally revealed, is required for the explanation or defense of a formally revealed truth. In turn, to show that a proposition is formally revealed, we must show that it is either contained in sacred Scripture or tradition, or else that it is logically implied by something contained therein (perhaps with the aid of naturally certain premises). Formally revealed propositions are *primary* objects of infallibility. However, even if a proposition isn't formally revealed, it is a *secondary* object of infallibility provided that it is necessary to explain or defend some formally revealed truth.[8] For each of the three claims contained in the proposed fifth Marian dogma, the focus of my theological analysis will be whether that claim is either a primary or a secondary object of infallibility.

8. For more on secondary objects of infallibility see Francis A. Sullivan, S.J., *Magisterium: Teaching Authority in the Catholic Church* (Eugene: Wipf & Stock Publishers, 2002) 131–38. Sullivan's book also offers useful accounts of the function of extraordinary magisterium, the ordinary and universal magisterium, the concept of infallibility, and a variety of related topics.

The contribution of philosophical analysis to the present inquiry is more complex. Philosophy is an exercise of natural human reason. As such, philosophy cannot prove propositions which are proper objects of infallibility, since the latter are not accessible to reason operating independently of revelation.[9] A philosophical argument might assist theology by adducing naturally certain reasons to think that some proposition is required for the explanation or defense of a formally revealed truth, and hence that the proposition is a secondary object of infallibility.[10] Even so, the proposition derives its truth not from the philosophical argument but from the formally revealed truth(s) it is required to explain or defend. Perhaps a more important role for philosophy in this context is to help us understand better what we believe on faith. Whereas theology explains *why* some proposition is true (i.e., because it is either formally revealed or required to explain or defend what is formally revealed), philosophy explains *how* the proposition is true by providing a viable model for comprehending it. For example, if the proposition that Mary is Mediatrix of all graces in a certain sense is a proper object of infallibility, it is helpful to have some positive idea of what it is like for such a thing to be true. As aids to understanding some proposition, various philosophical models may be constructed from different philosophical traditions: Scholastic, analytic, Continental, and so forth. Though I shall draw philosophical understanding primarily from the Scholastic tradition, I encourage other philosophers

9. Possible exceptions are the conclusions of traditional natural theology, such as that God exists, is unique, simple, endowed with will and intellect, and so forth. Such propositions might be formally revealed *and* capable of being corroborated by human reason operating independently of revelation.

10. Since most—if not all—philosophical arguments, no matter how rigorous, are subject to some degree of intellectual uncertainty, before such a proposition can be officially declared a secondary object of infallibility it must acquire the full theological certainty derived from a formal definition by the extraordinary magisterium or from a definitive teaching by the ordinary universal magisterium.

to plumb their own traditions for effective interpretive instruments. The more we have at our disposal, the better.

Much of the philosophical analysis contained in this book is difficult. Just as heat is a simple thing even though its thermodynamic explanation is not, so the philosophical models used to explicate truths of the faith can be quite complicated. Yet the reader should take comfort in the following thought. No matter how complicated a good philosophical analysis is, by persistently following it we eventually reach a juncture where the basic idea driving the analysis becomes crystal clear to us. We can then apply this insight to explicate earlier points in the analysis that struck us as obscure. Or if these obscure points are actually flaws, then perhaps we can see our way to an alternative and more satisfying philosophical analysis. I leave it to the reader to decide whether the philosophical analyses proffered in the present work are good ones, and whether there are preferable alternative solutions to the ones I propose. Each of my chapters is a foray on a theme that others may be able to develop differently.

Finally, what answers will be given to the theological and philosophical questions concerning the three claims contained in the proposed dogma? Regarding (C1), I will argue that no formal definition of Mary as Co-Redemptrix is justified at this time, nor is it likely that a formal definition will be justified at some future time. Regarding (C2), I will argue that no formal definition of Mary as Mediatrix of all graces is justified at this time, though in light of possible theological and philosophical development a formal definition might be justified at some future time, with potentially far-reaching consequences for the Church. Regarding (C3), I will argue that no formal definition of Mary as Advocate is necessary because the legitimate content of this claim is already fully embraced by the Church as formally revealed. Therefore, my general conclusion regarding the proposed fifth Marian dogma is that a formal definition of it is currently unjustified and will remain so, but that a formal definition of at least one of its constituent claims might become justified in the fullness of time.

CHAPTER 1

Mary as Co-Redemptrix Part I: Preserved from the Fall

Fr. John A. Hardon, S.J. defines the term "Co-Redemptrix" as follows:

> A title of the Blessed Virgin as co-operator with Christ in the work of human redemption. It may be considered an aspect of Mary's mediation in not only consenting to become the Mother of God but in freely consenting in his labors, sufferings, and death for the salvation of the human race.[1]

In the remainder of his entry for this term, Hardon writes:

> As Co-Redemptrix, she is in no sense equal to Christ in his redemptive activity, since she herself required redemption and in fact was redeemed by her Son. He alone merited man's salvation. Mary effectively interceded to obtain subjective application of Christ's merits to those whom the Savior had objectively redeemed.[2]

This second passage contains assertions which proponents of a fifth Marian dogma find objectionable. We shall return to these points of contention later. For now, let us focus on the first passage, since the claims it makes and distinctions it draws are accepted by all parties to the dispute.

---

1. *Pocket Catholic Dictionary* (New York: Doubleday, 1985) 94.
2. Ibid.

By "the work of human redemption" is meant the freeing of all human beings from the penalties due to Original Sin.[3] This work begins with the Incarnation of the Word in human flesh, in the person of Jesus Christ, and continues through Christ's ministry on Earth, culminating in his suffering and death on the Cross at Calvary. Mary first cooperates with Christ in the work of human redemption by freely consenting to become the Mother of God by the power of the Holy Spirit. Her initial consent is sometimes referred to as her "fiat." Mary subsequently cooperated with her Son throughout his earthly life by bringing him as an infant to be purified in the temple, raising him in holiness, and assisting him as an adult in his ministry. Finally, Mary cooperated with Christ by consenting to his suffering and death and experiencing intense maternal suffering on his behalf, sometimes referred to as the "transpiercing" or "transfixing" of her soul at Calvary.

Beginning in the early twentieth century, a number of papal documents include passages which focus on Mary's cooperation with Christ in the work of human redemption. In his 1904 encyclical *Ad Diem Illum* Pope Pius X writes:

> We are then, it will be seen, very far from attributing to the Mother of God a productive power of grace—a power which belongs to God alone. Yet, since Mary carries it over all in holiness and union with Jesus Christ, and has been associated with Jesus Christ in the work of redemption, she merits for us *de congruo*, in the language of theologians, what Jesus Christ merits for

---

3. It is Catholic teaching that while human beings do not inherit the personal guilt of the first sinner, they are liable to punishment for his sin in, the way that a person's heirs or teammates are liable to punishment for an infraction he committed even though they are not personally guilty of that infraction. In this sense all humans are subject to the penalties due to Original Sin unless they are redeemed.

> us *de condigno*, and she is the supreme Minister of the
> distribution of graces.[4]

The notions of merit *de condigno*, or condign merit, and merit *de congruo*, or congruous merit, will occupy us in the next chapter. In the passage above, the mind of Pius X does seem to be that in cooperating with Christ, Mary in some way co-merits what Christ merits for us—namely, our redemption from Original Sin.

Pope Benedict XV comes close to describing Mary as co-redeemer in his Apostolic Letter *Inter Soldalica* of March 22, 1918:

> She suffers with her suffering and dying son, almost as
> if she would have died herself. For the salvation of man-
> kind, she gave up her rights as the mother of her son and
> sacrificed him for the reconciliation of divine justice, as
> far as she was permitted to do. Therefore, one can say,
> she redeemed with Christ the human race.[5]

Benedict XV stops short of saying that Mary's suffering and sacrifice of her maternal rights in any way *merited* the salvation of mankind. Pope Pius XII, in his 1943 encyclical *Mystici Corporis*, understands Mary's maternal sacrifice as a kind of offering:

> It was she, the second Eve, who, free from all sin, and al-
> ways more intimately united with her Son, offered Him
> on Golgotha to the Eternal Father for all the children of
> Adam, sin-stained by his unhappy fall, and her mother's
> rights and her mother's love were included.[6]

Like Benedict XV, Pius XII does not speak of Mary's offering in terms of merit. Although he doesn't use the term "Co-Redemptrix," in his 1950 papal bull *Munificentissimus Deus*, in which he defines ex cathedra the dogma of the Assumption,

4. *Ad Diem Illum Laetissimum* 14.

5. *Inter Sodalicia* 181.

6. *Mystici Corporis* 110.

Pius XII does refer to Mary as "the noble associate of the divine Redeemer."[7]

Pope John Paul II used the term "Co-Redemptrix" in several addresses he made during his pontificate. In his General Audience of September 8, 1982 he said, "Mary, though conceived and born without the taint of sin, participated in a marvelous way in the suffering of her divine Son, in order to be Co-Redemptrix of humanity."[8] John Paul II does not elaborate upon the manner of Mary's participation in her Son's sufferings. On January 31, 1985, in Guayaquil, Ecuador, he remarked that "As she was in a special way close to the cross of her Son, she also had a privileged experience of his Resurrection. In fact, Mary's role as Co-Redemptrix did not cease with the glorification of her Son."[9] Again, the Holy Father does not expand upon the special way Mary was close to Jesus on the Cross or the privileged experience she had of his Resurrection. The term "Co-Redemptrix" also occurs in some of John Paul II's other addresses.[10]

What is the precise nature of Mary's cooperation with Christ in the work of human redemption? In cooperating with Christ, did she co-merit with him our salvation? In exactly what sense is Mary Co-Redemptrix? These deeper theological questions are left unanswered by the foregoing papal statements. Humbly and reverently, let us apply human reason in an attempt to find some answers.

---

7. *Munificentissimus Deus* 40.

8. *Insegnamenti di Giovanni Paolo II*, I/3 (1982) 404.

9. *Inseg* VIII/1 (1985) 318–19.

10. *Inseg* VII/2 (1984) 1151; *Inseg* VIII/1 (1985) 889–90; *Inseg* XIV/2 (1991) 756. All excerpts from John Paul II's addresses follow the translations found in Mark Miravalle, "Response to a Statement of an International Theological Commission of the Pontifical International Marian Academy" (1997) at http://www.voxpopuli.org/response_e.php (Endnotes).

DISAMBIGUATION AND THE ORDER
OF EVALUATION

We begin by distinguishing two senses in which Mary can be considered Co-Redemptrix:

(1) Mary is *instrumental Co-Redemptrix*, in that by virtue of her Immaculate Conception she cooperated preeminently with Christ by giving him a human body free from the penalties due to Original Sin which he then used to accomplish the work of human redemption.

(2) Mary is *meritorious Co-Redemptrix*, in that her maternal sufferings on behalf of her son's suffering and death co-merited with Christ human redemption.

One possible position is that Mary is neither instrumental Co-Redemptrix nor meritorious Co-Redemptrix. I will set this possibility aside, since even if the term "Co-Redemptrix" is rejected our faith teaches that, by her Immaculate Conception, Mary cooperated with Christ at least by giving him a body untainted by Original Sin. I will also set aside the possibility that Mary is only meritorious Co-Redemptrix, since no one who maintains that she is meritorious Co-Redemptrix denies that she is also instrumental Co-Redemptrix. We are then left with two possible theses:

(T1) Mary is instrumental Co-Redemptrix but not meritorious Co-Redemptrix.

(T2) Mary is both instrumental Co-Redemptrix and meritorious Co-Redemptrix.

Our disambiguation of "Co-Redemptrix" has ramifications for any proposed fifth Marian dogma proclaiming that Mary is Co-Redemptrix. The proposed dogma may be understood as proclaiming Mary to be merely instrumental Co-Redemptrix, or as proclaiming her also to be meritorious Co-Redemptrix.

Consequently, someone who denies (T2) may still advocate a fifth Marian dogma proclaiming (T1).[11]

These observations impose a certain order on our evaluation of the proposed dogma:

Stage A: Is there an adequate theological basis for the proposition that Mary is instrumental Co-Redemptrix?

Stage B: If so, then is there a viable philosophical model for the truth of this proposition?

Stage C: If so, then is this proposition sufficiently distinct from previous formal definitions or definitive teachings?

Stage D: Is the proposition that Mary is meritorious Co-Redemptrix sufficiently distinct from previous formal definitions or definitive teachings?

Stage E: If so, then is there an adequate theological basis for this proposition?

Stage F: If so, then is there a viable philosophical model for the truth of this proposition?

A necessary condition for the formal definition of a dogma containing (T1) to be justified is that there are affirmative answers to the questions at stages A through C and a negative answer to at least one question at stages D through F. A necessary condition for the formal definition of a dogma containing (T2) is that there are affirmative answers to the questions at all the stages from A to F. In either case, fulfillment of the requisite conditions isn't sufficient, because supportive Scriptural exegesis, ecclesiastical review, and most of all guidance by the Holy Spirit are also required before any such formal definition is justified.

11. Based on personal communication and study of the sources, my impression is that most, if not all, proponents of the proposed fifth Marian dogma interpret it as proclaiming (T2), not (T1). However, I may have overlooked proponents who advocate a dogma proclaiming (T1) rather than (T2). In any case, the latter is a logically possible view that a fully rigorous inquiry ought to address.

I leave these additional tasks to others who are better qualified to pursue them than I am. However, affirmative answers to the theological and philosophical questions are necessary before any formal definition of a dogma containing (T1) or (T2) is warranted. The reason is that any formally defined dogma should not only be suitably related to what we already believe on faith but also free from insuperable contradiction or obvious intellectual incoherence.

With these preliminaries in place, in this chapter we shall answer the questions at stages A through C to determine whether the positive necessary conditions for the formal definition of a dogma containing (T1) are met. In the next chapter we shall proceed to the questions at stages D through F to determine whether the remaining necessary conditions are met for the formal definition of a dogma containing (T2).

STAGE A

Is there an adequate theological basis for the proposition that Mary is instrumental Co-Redemptrix?

In the Introduction, we saw that one can establish an adequate theological basis for some proposition by showing either that the proposition is logically implied by formally revealed truths— possibly with the aid of naturally certain premises—or that the proposition is required for the explanation or defense of some formally revealed truth. In the first case, the proposition itself is also a formally revealed truth, albeit one that is implicit in the deposit of faith until the logical implication is established. In the second case, though not itself a formally revealed truth, the proposition is a so-called secondary object of infallibility.

Even if she had done nothing else to assist Jesus, to be instrumental Co-Redemptrix it is sufficient for Mary freely to give him a body exempt from the penalties due to Original Sin. The following argument is then available to the theologian:

(i) If Mary is conceived without Original Sin and if she freely consents to become the Mother of God by the power of the Holy Spirit, then she freely gives her Son a body exempt from Original Sin.

(ii) Mary is conceived without Original Sin.

(iii) Mary freely consents to become the Mother of God by the power of the Holy Spirit.

(iv) Therefore, Mary freely gives her Son a body exempt from Original Sin.

This argument is logically valid. The truth of premise (i) is guaranteed by the exercise of divine omnipotence through the Person of the Holy Spirit, together with divine assurance that the virginal conception to which Mary freely consented is brought to term. Premise (ii) is the doctrine of the Immaculate Conception, defined as a dogmatic truth by Pope Pius IX in 1854. The truth of premise (iii) is revealed by what sacred Scripture tells us in Luke 1:38 concerning Mary's reply to the angel Gabriel. As we noted, the truth of (iv) is sufficient for Mary to be instrumental Co-Redemptrix, though it is compatible with her continuing to fulfill this role by subsequently cooperating with Christ in a variety of ways during his earthly life. Consequently, an adequate theological basis exists for the proposition that Mary is instrumental Co-Redemptrix, since the proposition is a logical consequence of other formally revealed truths.

The proposition that Mary is instrumental Co-Redemptrix derives its theological basis largely from the dogma of the Immaculate Conception. Hence it is instructive to reflect upon the theological basis of the latter dogma.[12] This basis is not provided merely by Pius IX's solemn definition, but also by reflection on Christ as most perfect redeemer. Bl. John Duns Scotus

12. I do not rule out the possibility of an equally adequate theological basis for the dogma that is different from the Scotist one presented in the text.

takes it to be a naturally certain truth that the most perfect way possible to redeem humanity from Original Sin is to prevent at least one person from ever contracting Original Sin in the first place. Since Christ, who is God Himself in human flesh, is a most perfect redeemer, Christ redeems humanity in the most perfect way possible. Therefore, Scotus concludes, Christ prevents at least one person from ever contracting Original Sin. This form of redemption is known as *preservative*, and the sole person who receives it is the immaculately conceived Mary.[13]

Against Scotus's argument it might be objected that a yet more perfect way to redeem humanity would be to prevent not just one but many or even all persons from contracting Original Sin. The objection assumes that a redemption in which more than one person receives preservative redemption is more perfect than a redemption in which only one person receives preservative redemption—presumably because each act of preservative redemption increases the total value of the redemption of humanity.

In reply, a Scotist might challenge this assumption.[14] Specifically, the following scenario is logically possible: any act of ordinary redemption (in which a person who contracts Original Sin is freed from it[15]) possesses an infinite order of value V. Since sin is an infinite offense against God, it can only be redeemed by a redemption of infinite value. The total value of a redemption consisting of more than one act of ordinary redemption is still V.

13. See *Ordinatio* 3, dist. 3, q.1. Translated by Allan B. Wolter, O.F.M. in *Four Questions on Mary* (Saint Bonaventure, New York: The Franciscan Institute, 2000) 35–36. Later we shall return to the philosophical model Scotus provides of *how* Mary was preserved from Original Sin through Christ's foreseen merits.

14. Though the reply I present is not what Scotus explicitly says, I believe it is logically available to him or to those who consider themselves his intellectual followers.

15. The fruits of the redemption are typically applied to a particular person through the sacrament of baptism.

An analogy is the cardinality N of the set of positive whole numbers. This cardinality is shared by the set of negative whole numbers, the set of positive integers, the set of negative integers, and various other sets, so that the cardinality of a set consisting of the union of any of these sets is still N. Furthermore, any act of preservative redemption (in which a person is preserved from contracting Original Sin) possesses an infinite order of value R that is strictly greater than V. The total value of a redemption containing only one act of preservative redemption plus acts of ordinary redemption is greater than the total value of a redemption containing only acts of ordinary redemption ($R+V > V$), just as the cardinality of the set consisting of the negative real numbers and the positive whole numbers is greater than the cardinality of the set of positive whole numbers. However, no number of additional acts of preservative redemption increases the total value of a redemption containing at least one act of preservative redemption ($R+(R+V) = R+V$), just as the cardinality of the set consisting of the real numbers in the interval from -3 to -2, the real numbers in the interval from -1 to 0, and the positive whole numbers equals the cardinality of the set consisting of the real numbers in the interval from -1 to 0 and the positive whole numbers.[16] Since a total redemption in which more than one person is prevented from contracting Original Sin is *not* more prefect that a total redemption in which only one person is prevented from contracting Original Sin, in bestowing preservative redemption on only one person Christ does not fail to redeem humanity in the most perfect way possible. This result disarms the objection to Scotus's argument.[17]

16. Here I assume the truth of the widely accepted continuum hypothesis, according to which every non-denumerable set of real numbers has the same cardinality as the set of all real numbers, which is the continuum.

17. Would a redemption in which all persons receive preservative redemption be more perfect than a redemption in which only one person

So far the scenario described in the last paragraph is merely logical. Is there any reason to believe that it characterizes the actual economy of redemption, or that Mary is the sole person who receives preservative redemption? Scotus enunciates his famous "Marian Principle": "but if the authority of the Church or the authority of Scripture does not contradict such, *it seems probable that what is more excellent should be attributed to Mary*."[18] Far from being an ad hoc imposition, Scotus's Marian Principle has a Scriptural foundation in Luke 1:28, where the angel Gabriel addresses Mary as "favored one" or "full of grace." An alternate translation is "most highly favored daughter." These phrases strongly suggest that Mary possesses grace to the fullest extent possible for a normal human being (i.e., a human who, unlike the God-Man, is not also God). Since receiving preservative redemption is the greatest form of grace possible for a normal human being, Mary received preservative redemption. And in light of what we have learned concerning the orders of various types of redemption, there is no more perfect way of redeeming

---

receives preservative redemption while everyone else receives ordinary redemption? A Scotist may answer that because no number of additional acts of preservative redemption increases the total value of a redemption including just one act of preservative redemption, since $(R+R+\ldots+R)=R$, the total value of a universal preservative redemption remains R. Where $(R+V+\ldots+V)$ is a redemption in which only one person receives preservative redemption and everyone else receives ordinary redemption, $R \leq (R+V+\ldots+V)$. If R is less than $(R+V+\ldots+V)$, then the latter redemption is more perfect than a universal preservative redemption. If R equals $(R+V+\ldots+V)$, then a universal preservative redemption is no more perfect than a total redemption in which only one person receives preservative redemption and everyone else receives ordinary redemption, so that by redeeming humanity in the latter way rather than in the former way Christ does not fail to redeem humanity in a more perfect way. Since both ways are equally perfect, by redeeming humanity by preserving Mary from Original Sin and freeing everyone one else from it Christ redeems humanity as perfectly as possible.

18. Ibid., 45 in Wolter's translation.

humanity than preventing only Mary from contracting Original Sin and freeing every other normal human being from Original Sin already contracted. We may conclude that the dogma of the Immaculate Conception, and hence the proposition that Mary is instrumental Co-Redemptrix, is justified both scripturally and theologically.

The centrality of Scotus's Marian Principle to the foregoing theological justification of the dogma of the Immaculate Conception and the proposition that Mary is instrumental Co-Redemptrix should not be underestimated. For, as we shall see, proponents of a fifth Marian dogma may appeal to the Marian Principle to argue that being meritorious Co-Redemptrix should also be attributed to Mary because being both meritorious and instrumental Co-Redemptrix is more excellent than being only instrumental Co-Redemptrix. Our assessment of this argument must wait until the next chapter. Let us continue with the next stage in our evaluation of the instrumental Co-Redemptrix proposition.

STAGE B

Is there a viable philosophical model for the proposition that Mary is instrumental Co-Redemptrix?

Recall that the primary role of philosophy in the current context is to explain not *why* but *how* a given theological proposition is true by giving us a model that helps us to understand it better. Because Mary's cooperative acts were performed by a woman who was preserved from the taint of Original Sin from the moment of her conception, to understand how Mary is instrumental Co-Redemptix we must also understand how she was preserved from Original Sin. The classic philosophical explanation of Mary's preservative redemption is also due to Scotus:

> [I]t is evident that the door was open to her through
> the merits of Christ that were foreseen and accepted in

> a special way for this person, so that because of his pas-
> sion this person was never in a state of sin and hence
> there was no reason why the door was closed, although,
> by reason of origin, it would have been closed to her just
> as it was to others.[19]

According to Scotus, God foresaw that Christ was going to merit the redemption of humanity through his suffering and death on the Cross. God prevented Mary from ever contracting Original Sin by applying a portion of Christ's foreseen merits to her at the moment of her conception. Throughout her life Mary performed cooperative acts—such as consenting to become the Mother of God by the power of the Holy Spirit and thus giving Christ a human body untainted by Original Sin—while remaining in a state of grace that was conveyed upon her by Christ's foreseen merits.

To fill in this picture it will help to consider an analogy. Knowing that Aloysius will eventually write a great novel earning millions of dollars, I prevent Philomena, who would otherwise be imprisoned, from ever going to prison in exchange for a portion of Aloysius's foreseen earnings. Philomena subsequently retrieves pen and paper from a hiding place only she knows and gives them to Aloysius, who then writes his great novel and earns millions of dollars, including the portion I accept as payment for Philomena's freedom. Similarly, knowing that Christ will eventually merit the redemption of humanity through his Passion, God prevents Mary at her conception from incurring the debt of Original Sin in exchange for a portion of Christ's foreseen merits. Mary subsequently consents to give Christ the body which he then uses to merit the redemption of humanity, including the portion God accepts as payment for Mary's preservative redemption.

A weakness of the analogy is that it leaves open the possibility of Philomena earning her own release from prison. For suppose I know that Philomena herself will eventually write a

19. Ibid., 53 in Wolter's translation.

great novel earning millions of dollars. In light of this foreknowledge I prevent Philomena from ever going to prison in exchange for a portion of her foreseen earnings. She then retrieves pen and paper, writes the novel, and earns the full profit, a portion of which I accept as payment for her freedom. Yet clearly Mary cannot earn her own preservative redemption, "because Mary most of all needed Christ as a redeemer."[20]

The difference between these two cases, one might argue, is that the debt incurred by Original Sin cannot be redeemed by the foreseen merits of any merely human being. For this debt possesses an infinite order of negative value which can only be redeemed by a corresponding infinite order of positive value.[21] Indeed, we have seen that earning Mary's preservative redemption requires an infinite order of positive value R that is strictly greater than the infinite order of value V required to earn the ordinary redemption of someone who has contracted Original Sin. The acts of a divine being—or in the case of the God-Man, a being who is both human and divine—are necessary to earn the infinite order of positive value required for Mary's preservative redemption. In terms of our analogy, we might imagine that Philomena is permanently illiterate and that only Aloysius is brilliant enough to write the novel that will earn her freedom.

I conclude that there is a viable philosophical model for the dogma of the Immaculate Conception and, consequently, for the proposition that Mary is instrumental Co-Redemptrix. An interesting question arises. In the actual economy of redemption, does Christ merit preservative redemption for Mary, who then

20. Ibid., 49 in Wolter's translation.

21. If someone dies in Original Sin, then that person is denied the beatific vision for all eternity (unless God absolves the debt by bestowing absolute clemency). Although eternity is not an infinite temporal duration, to the extent that eternity can be measured it is infinite. Thus the debt which deprives even just one person of the beatific vision for all eternity must also infinite to the same degree—i.e., it must possess an infinite order of negative value. See footnote 15, chapter 2.

cooperates with Christ to co-merit the ordinary redemption of everybody else? Again, in terms of our analogy, the situation would be tantamount to a portion of Aloysius's foreseen earnings from a novel he will write being applied to prevent the imprisonment of Philomena, who then not only supplies Aloysius with pen and paper to write that novel but subsequently co-writes with him a second novel generating earnings which are used to purchase the release of prisoners who are already in jail.[22] Most, if not all, proponents of a fifth Marian dogma answer the question of whether Mary is also meritorious Co-Redemptrix affirmatively. This question will occupy us in the next chapter.

STAGE C

Is the proposition that Mary is instrumental Co-Redemptrix sufficiently distinct from previous formal definitions or definitive teachings?

We noted the close connection between the dogma of the Immaculate Conception and the proposition that Mary is instrumental Co-Redemptrix. The truth of the latter proposition logically follows from the truth of the dogma in conjunction with fundamental truths about God and Scriptural truths about Mary. In addition to freely giving Christ a body exempt from

22. Another possibility is that Philomena (Mary) cooperates with Aloysius (Christ) by co-writing with him the book (consenting to his sacrifice and suffering with him), some of whose earnings (merits) are applied to purchase her freedom (preservative redemption). In what follows I will not consider this possibility, since every proponent I know of the proposition that Mary is meritorious Co-Redemptrix maintains that Mary cooperates with Christ in earning only the ordinary redemption of other humans, not her own preservative redemption. However, the points I shall make apply to this possibility, as well as to the standard interpretation of the meritorious Co-Redemptrix proposition.

Original Sin, Mary's being instrumental Co-Redemptrix consists in her raising Christ in holiness, assisting him in his adult ministry, consenting to his suffering and death on the Cross, and experiencing maternal suffering on his behalf. All these truths are explicitly taught by sacred Scripture and/or sacred tradition. In short, the proposition that Mary is instrumental Co-Redemptrix is already an explicit element in the deposit of faith. Apparently, then, there is no need for any formal definition of a dogma containing this proposition, and hence for a formal definition containing the thesis that Mary is *only* instrumental Co-Redemptrix.

It might be replied that although describing Mary as instrumental Co-Redemptrix adds nothing new to what is already explicitly in the deposit of faith, it is useful to have a single term designating Mary's various acts of cooperating with Christ in his redemptive work. This usefulness gives some point to a formal definition attributing to Mary the title "Co-Redemptrix" in a merely instrumental sense.

However, we must weigh the usefulness of any such term against its potential to mislead and to distort the truth. Literally speaking, "Co-Redemptrix" doesn't mean "one who assists another who redeems" but "one who redeems with another," just as "co-writer" doesn't mean "one who assists another who writes" but "one who writes with another." If Philomena merely supplies Aloysius with pen and paper he uses to write a novel, then it is deeply misleading and in fact literally false to say that Philomena is co-writer. Similarly, if Mary merely gives Christ a body exempt from Original Sin which he uses to redeem humanity, then it is misleading and literally false to say that Mary is Co-Redemptrix.

The title would be neither misleading nor false if, in co-operating with Christ, Mary also co-redeemed the rest of humanity by co-meriting their salvation. To determine whether she did requires an evaluation of the proposition that Mary is meritorious Co-Redemptrix. That evaluation is the task of the next chapter. For now, we may conclude that any formal definition containing the thesis that Mary is merely instrumental Co-Redemptrix is unwarranted. Everything legitimately asserted by this thesis is already explicitly in the deposit of faith without the problematic title.

CHAPTER 2

Mary as Co-Redemptrix Part II:
Getting Marian Mathematics Right

For Mary to be meritorious Co-Redemptrix, it is not sufficient that she cooperate with Christ in his work of human redemption. She must also co-merit with him human redemption.
In the most developed version of the meritorious Co-Redemptrix
proposition familiar to me, some of the foreseen merits merited
by Christ's suffering and death are first applied to earn Mary's
preservative redemption. Mary's maternal sufferings on her Son's
behalf at Calvary (and perhaps other meritorious acts she performs) then earn at least some merits which, combined with the
merits earned by Christ's suffering and death, earn the ordinary
redemption of every human being besides her.[1] Furthermore,
the merits supposedly earned by Mary's maternal sufferings are
strictly less than the merits earned by Christ's sufferings and
death, since as meritorious Co-Redemptrix Mary is subordinate

---

1. For example, see the remarks of Fr. Angelo Geiger at http:/www
.airmaria.com/2008/04/23/ideo-dr-mark-miravalle-marycast-16-finding
-of-jesus-in-the-temple/. Fr. Geiger bases his position on the views expressed by Rev. Peter Damian M. Fehlner, F.F.I. in "Immaculata Mediatrix—Toward a Dogmatic Definition of the Coredemption." Printed
in *Mary, CoRedemptrix, Mediatrix, Advocate, Theological Foundations II:
Papal, Pneumatological, Ecumenical*, ed. Mark I. Miravalle (Goleta, CA:
Queenship Publishing Company, 1997). Fehlner's essay can be found
online at http://www.christendom-awake.org/pages/marian/5thdogma/
fehlner1-1.htm (This link brings up Part I; at the bottom of the last page
there is a link to Part II).

to Christ as principle Redeemer.[2] Proponents of a fifth Marian dogma thus favor a formal definition including (T2): Mary is both instrumental and meritorious Co-Redemptrix.

In this chapter we shall proceed with our overall evaluation of the claim that Mary is Co-Redemptrix by considering whether the proposition that Mary is meritorious Co-Redemptrix is theologically warranted, philosophically viable, and doctrinally distinct from previous dogmas. We begin with the last question.

STAGE D

Is the proposition that Mary is meritorious Co-Redemptrix sufficiently distinct from previous formal definitions or definitive teachings?

The four current Marian dogmas do not logically imply that Mary literally co-merited with Christ our redemption. They cannot, because whether Mary co-merited our redemption depends on acts of her free will which are not necessarily determined by her Divine Maternity, Perpetual Virginity, Immaculate Conception, or Assumption. Nor is the meritorious Co-Redemptrix proposition required for the explanation or defense of any of the previous dogmas, since they have been adequately explained and defended without recourse to this proposition. Therefore, the proposition that Mary is meritorious Co-Redemptrix is sufficiently distinct from previous formal definitions or definitive teachings. If true, it expresses an important fact about her role in the economy of redemption that is not expressed by current Marian dogmas.

Moreover, if the proposition that Mary is meritorious Co-Redemptrix is true, then so is the proposition that she is

2. See ibid. at 13 in the online version: "with Christ *and under Christ* Mary forms, in virtue of their joint predestination, a single redemptive personality" (emphasis added).

instrumental Co-Redemptrix, provided that the latter is suitably interpreted. For then Mary is literally Co-Redemptrix, and she also cooperates preeminently with Christ by giving him a body exempt from Original Sin which he uses to accomplish his part of the ordinary redemption of every human being besides her. In short, Mary is both instrumental and Co-Redemptrix; therefore, she is instrumental Co-Redemptrix.[3] The truth of the meritorious Co-Redemptrix proposition, together with the fact that Mary cooperates with Christ in the work of human redemption by giving him a body exempt from Original Sin and performing various other acts, guarantees the truth of (T2). Thus the appropriateness of the formal definition of a dogma containing the thesis that Mary is both instrumental and meritorious Co-Redemptrix hinges on whether there is an adequate theological basis for the proposition that she is meritorious Co-Redemptrix, and also whether there is a viable philosophical model for the truth of this same proposition. Before we resume our evaluation, let us first review a central distinction between types of merit.

DISAMBIGUATION: CONDIGN VERSUS CONGRUOUS MERIT

Being exempted from the penalties due to Original Sin—or in Mary's case, being prevented from ever incurring these penalties—is a divine gift, or grace. Christ merited this grace for us (or perhaps co-merited it with Mary) by suffering and dying on the Cross. This grace is applied to us if we receive the sacrament of baptism and have faith in Christ as our Lord and Savior. Christ solely merited for Mary the grace of being preserved from Original Sin, and through the foreseen merits of Christ's Passion this grace is applied to her from the moment of her conception.

3. Equivalently, the definition could stipulate that "Co-Redemptrix" is to mean "co-merits with Christ the ordinary redemption of other humans and is also preeminently instrumental in helping Christ accomplish his part in ordinary redemption of every human besides her."

When X *condignly* merits something from Y, as a matter of commutative justice Y has an obligation to reward X with what X has merited. For example, someone who performs a service for me when we are both under contract condignly merits my payment for his service as we agreed in the contract. The possibility of condign merit presupposes equality between the one who merits and the one who rewards. Both the person who performs the service and I are human beings who are equal before the law and treated as such by our legally binding contract. As the God-Man, Christ is equal to God because, in addition to being human, he *is* God. Hence when he consents to suffer and die for our sins, Christ condignly merits from God our redemption from Original Sin.

On the other hand, when X *congruously* merits something from Y, it is appropriate, yet not strictly required by commutative justice, that Y reward X with what X has merited. For example, a waiter who serves me dinner congruously merits a gratuity from me, in that although I am not obliged to reward him, it is highly fitting that I do so. The possibility of congruous merit does not presuppose equality between the one who merits and the one who rewards. In the service economy, the waiter is not my equal because I am the customer. Even so, this inequality does not render it impossible for him to merit something from me congruously.

A human being who has been exempted from the penalties due to Original Sin is redeemed, or in a state of sanctity. As such, it is possible for her to merit certain rewards from God either condignly or congruously. By herself, she can never be God's equal. But given that Christ has redeemed her and that God has promised to reward those who, once redeemed, remain in His friendship, if she preserves her sanctity by performing acts of prayer, penance, and devotion, then she condignly merits from God the glory of eternal life with Him. His fidelity to His promises and her virtuous acts of free will oblige Him to bestow this reward upon her. A human being in a state of sanctity can also congruously merit certain rewards from God. An example is when she prays that someone to whom the grace of redemption has not been applied by baptism nonetheless receive this grace. Commutative justice does not oblige God to grant her prayer. Yet unless there is some impediment in the recipient, such as consciousness of a mortal sin he has committed, it is highly fitting for God to grant her prayer by bestowing the first grace upon him.[4]

By virtue of the foreseen merits earned by Christ's suffering and death and applied to her from the moment of her conception, Mary was prevented from incurring the penalties of Original Sin. Moreover, she remained free from all sin, mortal or venial, for the entirety of her life on earth.[5] Thus throughout her earthly life Mary remained in a state of sanctity, and hence could merit either condignly or congruously from God. The question before us is whether Mary is meritorious Co-Redemptrix for the reason that she co-merited with Christ, either condignly or congruously, the ordinary redemption of every other human being. Presently we shall narrow down this question. With the distinction between condign and congruous merit firmly in mind, we may proceed with our evaluation of the proposition that Mary is meritorious Co-Redemptrix.

4. See *Summa Theologiae* 1a q.114 a.6, where St. Thomas Aquinas argues that someone can merit the first grace for another congruously, though not condignly. An English translation may be found online at http://www.newadvent.org/summa/2114.htm. All of q.114 is pertinent to the topic of merit in the order of grace.

5. See Pius IX, *Ineffabilis Deus*: DS2803; Council of Trent: DS 1573. These references are taken from *Catechism of the Catholic Church* (New York: Doubleday, 1995) note 306 to section 411 (at 116 in the text).

STAGE E

Is there an adequate theological basis for the proposition that Mary is meritorious Co-Redemptrix?

One might be tempted to think that the theological adequacy of the meritorious Co-Redemptrix proposition has already been established by the numerous papal statements quoted in the previous chapter:

> We are then, it will be seen, very far from attributing to the Mother of God a productive power of grace—a power which belongs to God alone. Yet, since Mary carries it over all in holiness and union with Jesus Christ, and has been associated with Jesus Christ in the work of redemption, she merits for us *de congruo*, in the language of theologians, what Jesus Christ merits for us *de condigno*, and she is the supreme Minister of the distribution of graces (Pius X).

> She suffers with her suffering and dying son, almost as if she would have died herself. For the salvation of mankind, she gave up her rights as the mother of her son and sacrificed him for the reconciliation of divine justice, as far as she was permitted to do. Therefore, one can say, she redeemed with Christ the human race (Benedict XV).

> It was she, the second Eve, who, free from all sin, and always more intimately united with her Son, offered Him on Golgotha to the Eternal Father for all the children of Adam, sin-stained by his unhappy fall, and her mother's rights and her mother's love were included (Pius XII).

> Mary, though conceived and born without the taint of sin, participated in a marvelous way in the suffering of her divine Son, in order to be Co-Redemptrix of humanity . . . As she was in a special way close to the cross of her Son, she also had a privileged experience of his

> Resurrection. In fact, Mary's role as Co-Redemptrix did
> not cease with the glorification of her Son (John Paul II).

Don't these statements and other papal references to Mary as "Co-Redemptrix" provide ample justification for a formal definition that includes the proposition that Mary is meritorious Co-Redemptrix?

It should be noted that not all of these papal statements unambiguously declare Mary to be meritorious Co-Redemptrix. Pius X's statement certainly does by asserting that Mary congruously merited our redemption, and Benedict XV comes close by asserting that she co-redeemed with Christ the human race. However, the remaining statements do not describe Mary in these terms. Taken as a whole, it is far from clear that these papal statements express a unified theology of Mary as meritorious Co-Redemptrix, rather than a plurality of theological perspectives on Mary's role in the economy of redemption.

More importantly, even if one or more of these papal statements unambiguously assert that Mary is meritorious Co-Redemptrix, that fact alone does not constitute an adequate theological basis for the proposition. These statements are teachings of the ordinary magisterium. Something taught by the ordinary magisterium (e.g., in papal addresses or encyclicals, in documents issued by individual bishops or groups of bishops, by an ecumenical council when it is not officially defining doctrine, or even by the ordinary and universal magisterium when it is not setting forth a doctrine as something to be held definitively) is not automatically a dogma of faith. Hence from the fact that the ordinary magisterium has spoken of Mary as meritorious Co-Redemptrix, it does not follow that this proposition has been infallibly taught or that it should be so taught, either as a primary or a secondary object of infallibility. Like other statements of the ordinary magisterium, such statements do not demand an assent of faith (*de fide*). At most they demand *obsequium religiosum*, or religious submission of will and intellect, to a degree less than the *obsequium religiosum* demanded of us in with regard to a secondary object of infallibility.[6] The degree of *obsequium religiosum* demanded of us with regard to some statement of the ordinary magisterium requires that we take the statement very seriously, examine our consciences for any unreasonable degree of obstinacy, and endeavor to remain open-minded in our consideration of the statement. Having satisfied these conditions, it is only if we remain unable to rid ourselves of all doubts about the statement's truth that we are entitled to withhold our full assent from it.

Although the foregoing papal statements of the ordinary magisterium do not provide an adequate theological basis for the proposition that Mary is meritorious Co-Redemptrix, our discussion in the last chapter of the Marian Principle of Duns Scotus suggests a more forceful line of argument. The suggestion is that the same principle can be used to justify, not only the proposition that Mary is meritorious Co-Redemptrix, but also the thesis (T2) that she is both meritorious Co-Redemptrix and instrumental Co-Redemptrix. For, assuming the truth of Scotus's Marian Principle, the proponent of (T2) may argue as follows:

(i) Whatever is more excellent should be attributed to Mary so long as it does not contradict the authority of the Church or the authority of Scripture (Scotus's Marian Principle).

(ii) It is more excellent that Mary be meritorious and instrumental Co-Redemptrix than that she be merely instrumental Co-Redemptrix (i.e., co-meriting with Christ the ordinary redemption of every other human being and also cooperating with Christ by giving him a body exempt from Original Sin and performing various other acts is more excellent

6. In the latter case, one should give full assent to the doctrine as something required to explain or defend the faith. Yet since the doctrine is not a formally revealed truth in the deposit of faith, strictly speaking it does not require an assent of *faith*. Even so, the assent it requires is no less full than an assent of faith. For more discussion see Sullivan, 162–66.

than merely cooperating with him in the aforementioned manner).

(iii) Mary's being meritorious and instrumental Co-Redemptrix does not contradict the authority of the Church or the authority of Scripture.

(iv) Therefore, being meritorious and instrumental Co-Redemptrix should be attributed to Mary.

This argument is logically valid. As we saw in the last chapter, there is a Scriptural foundation for the truth of (i), indicating that Scotus's Marian Principle is more than a mere speculative hypothesis. I will return to premise (ii) below.

What of premise (iii)? It might be objected that Mary's being both meritorious and instrumental Co-Redemptrix contradicts the authority of Scripture. For Mary's being meritorious Co-Redemptrix requires that she co-redeem with Christ every human being besides herself. Yet in 1 Timothy 2:5 we read that Christ is the one mediator between God and humanity, which seems to preclude the possibility of anyone else co-redeeming with him the human race, even Mary. Attributing the role of meritorious Co-Redemptrix to Mary seems to compromise Christ's role as the sole mediator.

A proponent of (T2) might counter that there is an important sense in which Christ is the sole mediator even if Mary co-redeems with him every human being besides herself. Specifically, being a mediator can be understood as being the ultimate arbiter who brings about a settlement between God and humanity by performing certain actions which not only earn the preservative redemption of at least one person but which also co-merit with that person's actions the ordinary redemption of everybody else. Christ alone has this property; therefore, Christ alone is mediator in this sense.[7] Since it is possible to understand "mediator" in

---

7. Here I am using "mediator" in a sense that is distinct from the male counterpart of "Mediatrix." The concept expressed by the latter term will be the focus of chapter 3.

the verse quoted from St. Paul in such terms, Mary's being meritorious and instrumental Co-Redemptrix is compatible with the verse in question, and thus does not contradict the authority of Scripture (at least not for the reasons given so far). Further assessment of premise (iii) requires the sort of Scriptural exegesis that lies beyond the scope of our analysis. So let us grant the provisional truth of (iii) and examine premise (ii) more closely.

The truth of premise (ii) seems obvious. Cooperating with Christ by giving him a body exempt from Original Sin and performing various other acts is certainly good, indeed excellent. So is co-meriting with Christ the ordinary redemption of other human beings. Intuitively, then, doing both is better or more excellent than doing only the first. However, this intuitive argument assumes the philosophical coherence of Mary's co-redeeming with Christ the ordinary redemption of every human being besides herself. If it turns out that Mary's being meritorious Co-Redemptrix is philosophically incoherent, then the good of her co-meriting adds no more to the good of her merely cooperating than 0 adds to 1. No doubt Scotus understands "excellent" to apply only to things which make basic sense. Alternatively, we can highlight the importance of philosophical considerations by slightly reformulating the argument:

(i)   What is more excellent should be attributed to Mary so long as it does not contradict the authority of the Church or the authority of Scripture and is philosophically coherent (modified Marian Principle).

(ii) It is more excellent that Mary be meritorious and instrumental Co-Redemptrix.

(iii) Mary's being meritorious and instrumental Co-Redemptrix does not contradict the authority of the Church or the authority of Scripture.

(iv) Mary's being meritorious and instrumental Co-Redemptrix is philosophically coherent.

(v) Therefore, being meritorious and instrumental Co-Redemptrix should be attributed to Mary.

In the present context, the philosophical coherence of a proposition or thesis does not consist in there being a proof of it from premises which are all naturally certain, but simply in there being a viable philosophical model enabling us to understand it so far as we are humanly able. Thus attention shifts to premise (iv); more precisely, since the fact that Mary cooperated with Christ by giving him a body exempt from Original Sin and performing various other acts is not under dispute, attention shifts to the question of whether the proposition that Mary is meritorious Co-Redemptrix is philosophically coherent. We conclude this section with the conditional conclusion that if the meritorious Co-Redemptrix proposition is philosophically coherent, then there is an adequate theological basis for (T2).

STAGE F

Is there a viable philosophical model for the proposition that Mary is meritorious Co-Redemptrix?

Earlier we noted that the question of whether Mary is meritorious Co-Redemptrix amounts to the question of whether she merited with Christ, either condignly or congruously, the ordinary redemption of every other human being. We begin our philosophical analysis by narrowing down this question.

Because she remained in a state of sanctity from the moment of her conception onward, during her earthly life Mary was capable of meriting either condignly or congruously from God. Pius X asserts that, in fact, she merited congruously for us what Christ merited condignly for us—namely, our redemption. Granting that Christ condignly merits the ordinary redemption of every other human besides Mary, is it possible for Mary to merit this same redemption, only congruously instead of condignly?

It is difficult to see how. An analogy will help bring out the problem. Imagine that Cyrus has been imprisoned by the king for committing a crime. We may also imagine that his punishment includes him and his heirs being deprived of their estate. The prince Amicus approaches the king and offers to toil in the fields for twenty years in exchange for Cyrus' release and the restoration of his estate. Being just and merciful, the king agrees to this arrangement. Prince Amicus proceeds to toil in the fields for twenty years, at the end of which time the king honors their agreement by releasing Cyrus and restoring his estate to him and his heirs. Amicus condignly merits from the king Cyrus's release and restoration. Now, suppose that while Amicus is toiling in the fields, his mother Martina kneels at the city gate every day and suffers on her son's behalf. Certainly the king may feel pity for Martina. He may even be moved to send her food and water, some of which she shares with others who are in need. Yet she does not in any sense merit Cyrus's release and restoration. She does not merit it condignly; only Amicus does by toiling in the field for twenty years. Nor does she merit it even congruously. For once the king confirms that Amicus has toiled in the fields for twenty years, he releases Cyrus from prison and restores his estate. Nothing else concerning Cyrus's release and restoration is left to be merited congruously by Martina. She may have congruously merited *other* rewards from the king, such as food and water.[8] But whatever she merits congruously does not pertain per se to the release and restoration of Cyrus.

One might try to defend the assertion that Christ condignly merited our redemption while Mary congruously merited it by

8. Given that Mary may and no doubt did congruously merit graces for us, and that Christ condignly merited our redemption, which is also a grace, a conservative reading of Pius X's assertion is that both Mary and Christ merit graces for us, he condignly and she congruously, though the graces they merit aren't the same. In particular, she doesn't congruously merit the redemption he condignly merits.

postulating in the economy of redemption a certain amalgam of grace. The idea is that, although the graces condignly merited by Christ's Passion are sufficient to earn our redemption, the graces congruously merited by Mary's maternal sufferings constitute a superabundant addition to the former graces, so that the total amalgam of grace (graces condignly merited by Christ plus graces congruously merited by Mary) as a matter of fact earns our redemption.[9] This amalgam could be compared to my being able to lift the table by myself but allowing you to help me, so that in fact we both lift the table. However, from the lifting analogy it immediately becomes clear what is wrong about the amalgam of grace idea. When you and I lift the table, our exertions combine to form a common action that causes the desired effect. Without this common action, our separate exertions accomplish nothing. By contrast, Christ's and Mary's sufferings on Calvary remain entirely distinct. They do not literally combine into a common suffering that accomplishes the desired end of meriting our redemption. Hence there is no amalgam of grace here.[10]

Accordingly, whether Mary is meritorious Co-Redemptrix boils down to whether Mary condignly merited with Christ the

9. We can speak of a plurality of graces merited by Christ or by Mary to the extent that what is merited may be applied separately to a number of human beings.

10. Let Q be the total value represented in numeric terms of what Amicus condignly merits. A somewhat different possibility is if the king graciously sets aside some portion P of Q, where P<Q, and accepts Martina's suffering on behalf of Amicus as having a meritorious value M that is strictly equal to the P, which the king then substitutes for the subtracted portion to attain a total merit equal to the original value Q. It should be noted that in such a case, by virtue of the king's gracious acceptance Martina condignly merits with Amicus, albeit in a manner subordinate to her son's meritorious actions, Cyrus's release and restoration. We shall next consider whether this possibility is applicable to Christ and Mary in the work of ordinary human redemption.

ordinary redemption of every other human being. In considering this question, it is crucial to keep three points in mind.

First, if Mary condignly merited with Christ our ordinary redemption, then the meritorious value of her co-redemptive acts (e.g., her maternal sufferings) must be strictly less than that of Christ's co-redemptive acts (his suffering and death on the Cross). For if the value of her acts were either greater than or equal to the value of his acts, then a non-divine being would be equal or even be superior to a divine being in accomplishing the work of ordinary redemption, which is absurd. Proponents of the meritorious Co-Redemptrix proposition acknowledge this point by attributing *de digno* merit to Mary's acts, a subordinate form of condign merit.[11] As such, the value of her co-redemptive acts must be greater than zero yet less than the value of Christ's co-redemptive acts.

Second, it might be worried that attributing *any* meritorious value to Mary's acts derogates from Christ. Because Christ is divine, the total meritorious value of his Passion is $(R+V+\ldots+V)$, where R is the value applied to earn Mary's preservative redemption and each V in $(V+\ldots+V)$ is the value applied to earn the ordinary redemption of a human being besides Mary. On the model we gave in chapter 1, $(V+\ldots+V) = V$ itself, so that $(R+V+\ldots+V) = (R+V)$. If Mary's acts contribute anything to Christ's work of ordinary redemption, then it seems that when he earns her preservative redemption, the value subtracted from $(R+V)$ must actually be greater than R enough to reduce $(R+V)$ to some positive value strictly less than V. Let this subtracted value be M. The worry here is that the value of Mary's co-redemptive acts must equal M to restore the original value V; otherwise, her acts contribute nothing to the ordinary redemptive value of Christ's passion. But then Christ by himself is incapable of meriting both Mary's preservative redemption and our ordinary redemption, which derogates from his divinity.

11. For example, see Fehlner, 9.

A proponent might address this worry by stressing that Christ's divinity guarantees that his Passion earns not only Mary's preservative redemption R but also our ordinary redemption V. Yet precisely because he is God, Christ can also decide to set aside some portion M of V such that $(V-M) < V$, allowing Mary to perform co-redemptive acts with the value of M to restore the original value V. Christ could have allowed his suffering and death to earn Mary's preservative redemption as well as our ordinary redemption, but he elects to earn Mary's preservative redemption and then to let co-redeem *de digne* with him our ordinary redemption.[12]

Third, recall from our discussion in chapter one that both R and V are infinite values, though the infinite value of R is strictly greater than the infinite value of V, just as the infinite cardinality of the set of real numbers is greater than the infinite cardinality of the set of natural numbers. These respective values must be positively infinite if they are to redeem the negatively infinite value of the debt of Original Sin that is or might be incurred by a person. Furthermore, if subtracting the value M from V is to equal some value strictly less than V, then the value of M must also be positively infinite. For subtracting a finite value from an infinite value still yields an infinite value, just as the cardinality of the set of natural numbers excluding those between 1 and 100 still equals the cardinality of the set of natural numbers. Thus subtracting M from V to obtain some finite value is analogous to excluding from the set of natural numbers the set of negative integers and the set of positive integers greater than 100 to obtain a set—the natural numbers from 0 to 100—the cardinality of which is finite.

With these points in mind, suppose that Christ elects to set aside some portion M of V. Setting aside this portion allows

12. I am ascribing this election to the God-Man. However, it could also be ascribed to the eternal Word or to some other Person of the Trinity.

for the possibility of a *de digne* co-redeemer who genuinely contributes to earning our ordinary redemption only if $(V-M) < V$, which in turn is possible only if the value of M is positively infinite. For Mary to co-merit *de digne* with Christ our ordinary redemption by helping him restore the original value V, then, the value of her meritorious acts must equal M. But since the value of M must be positively infinite, the value of Mary's meritorious acts must also be positively infinite. And it is impossible for the meritorious acts of any merely human being to have a positively infinite value. Only the acts of a divine being can. Therefore, it is impossible that Mary co-merit *de digne* with Christ the ordinary redemption of every other human being.

One response to the foregoing proof might be to question the premise that only the acts of a divine being can have positively infinite value. This premise is intuitively appealing, but is there any more substantive reason for it? I believe there is. Consider some act that has a positively infinite value, such as meriting the ordinary redemption of the infant Sal. The value earned by this act can be construed as consisting of infinitely many value units $v_1, v_2, \ldots$ making up the total infinite value V. Thus the agent who performs this act is capable of immediately earning infinitely many value units all at once. The same principle that Duns Scotus applies to the order of knowledge (viz., that an intellect capable of immediately knowing infinitely many things all at once must be infinite) and to the order of power (viz., that a power capable of immediately causing infinitely many things all at once must be infinite) can be applied to the order of merit: an agent capable of immediately earning infinitely many value units all at once must be infinite.[13] It would seem that a finite being could earn infinitely many value units only by acting for

13. For Scotus's application of the principle to the orders of knowledge and causal power see *De primo principio*, 4.48 and 4.70, respectively. Translated by Allan B. Wolter, O.F.M., as *A Treatise on God as First Principle* (Chicago: Franciscan Herald Press, 1966).

an infinite length of time, which would require the being's existence to be prolonged supernaturally. Obviously such a situation does not apply to Mary, whose allegedly co-redemptive acts took place only during her earthly life.[14]

Another possible response to the proof is that the value V applied to earn our ordinary redemption is actually finite, so that the portion M which Christ elects to set aside from V need not be positively infinite. The trouble with such a suggestion is that if the debt of Original Sin incurred by even one person, let alone all of humanity, has an infinitely negative value, then the value V applied to redeem us from this debt must be positively infinite in at least the same order of infinity. A positive finite value M added to only a positive finite value for V can never earn the infinitely positive value required to cancel the infinitely negative value of this debt.[15]

14. Supposing that Mary earns infinitely many value units by performing infinitely many co-redemptive acts during an infinite length of time creates a cascade of absurd consequences. Since her earthly life was only a finite length of time, Mary must perform co-redemptive acts after her death. Either these acts involve suffering or they do not. If her acts involve suffering, then either Mary suffers in Heaven, which is false because there is no suffering in Heaven, or Mary is in Purgatory or in Hell for an infinite length of time, which is also false. If her post-mortem co-redemptive acts do not involve suffering, it follows not only that we haven't yet been redeemed, since Mary is Heaven is still performing her co-redemptive acts, but also that we will never be redeemed, since an infinite length of time must elapse before Mary completes her co-redemptive acts.

15. The infinitely negative value of Original Sin need not be understood in retributive terms as a *debt* owed to God that one cannot pay back, but as the *loss* of something having infinitely positive value that one cannot regain on one's own: namely, eternal life with God. The nature of damnation, the eternal fate of those who are never redeemed from Original Sin because they reject Christ, lies beyond the scope of this work and deserves further study. For now I will make the following observation. A student who refuses to cooperate with an instructor to

In passing I mention Scotus's view (for example, in *Ordinatio* 3, dist. 19) that the total value of Christ's Passion is finite, including the value V applied to earn our ordinary redemption. Scotus defends an acceptance theory of the Atonement, according to which V earns our redemption simply because God accepts V as satisfaction for our being in a state of Original Sin. If V has only a finite value, then a Scotist might argue that Christ could set aside some finite portion M of V and allow Mary to perform meritorious acts with the value M which, when added to (V-M), restores the original finite value V that is accepted by God to earn our redemption. Mary could then co-merit *de digne* with Christ our ordinary redemption. Yet what reason is there to think that the total value of Christ's Passion is finite? Scotus suggests that Christ's Passion is permissively caused by Christ's humanity, not by his divinity. Since his humanity is finite, and since the meritorious acts permissively caused by a finite being must also be finite, the total value of Christ's Passion must also be finite. This reason is unsatisfactory, however, because Christ's Passion is permissively caused not only by his humanity but also by his divinity united to his human nature to form one person who, qua divine, is infinite. Thus the total value of meritorious acts permissively caused by this infinite being must also be infinite.

I suspect that Scotus's real reason for thinking that the total value of Christ's Passion is finite has to do with Scotus's understanding of predestination. Intuitively, something is infinite only if it is unlimited in any way. Because God doesn't apply the merits of Christ's Passion to everyone but only to the elect, the total value of Christ's Passion is limited, and hence is finite rather than infinite. The problem with Mary being meritorious Co-Redemptrix on this predestinationist scheme is that what

---

pass an exam by a certain deadline may lose the opportunity to earn a degree which the university is not obliged to offer the student again. Similarly, a sinner who refuses to accept Christ may forever lose eternal glory which God is not obliged to offer the sinner again.

makes the total value of Christ's Passion, including V, finite is simply the fact that God applies V only to the elect, who thereby receive ordinary redemption. Thus there is no place for Mary to co-merit *de digne* their ordinary redemption, for it has already been entirely merited by the value V included in Christ's Passion and applied only to the elect through divine predestination. If it is said that God could apply the total value of Christ's Passion and the total value of Mary's cooperation only to the elect, I reply that since both values are equally limited by being applied only to the elect they are finite to exactly the same extent, and thus equal—which cannot be the case, for Mary's merit must be subordinate to Christ's.

I conclude that the proposition that Mary is meritorious Co-Redemptrix is philosophically incoherent. More cautiously, we may say that the proposition has not been shown to be philosophically coherent. In light of the conditional conclusion reached at the end of the previous section, a corollary is that (T2)—the thesis that Mary is both instrumental and meritorious Co-Redemptrix—has not been shown to have an adequate theological basis. Moreover, in chapter 1 we concluded that (T1)—the thesis that Mary is merely instrumental Co-Redemptrix—is not sufficiently distinct from previous formal definitions or definitive teachings and also risks being misleading and false. Since (T1) and (T2) exhaust the interpretive options for (C1)—the claim that Mary is Co-Redemptrix because she cooperates preeminently with Christ is the work of human redemption—no formal definition of a dogma containing this claim is justified at this time. Nor is it likely to become justified, given the apparent decisiveness of the considerations which have been presented. All that is legitimately asserted in (C1) is already explicitly taught by the Church without the problematic title "Co-Redemptrix."

CHAPTER 3

Mary as Mediatrix of All Graces:
Reflecting upon the Mirror of Justice

W<small>E HAVE</small> completed the first third of our overall evaluation of the proposed fifth Marian dogma. In this chapter we turn to the second claim it contains:

(C2) Mary is Mediatrix of all graces because she mediates any and all graces merited by Christ which are bestowed upon us.

Unlike with the Co-Redemptrix claim, the prospect of justifying a formal definition containing the Mediatrix claim is more favorable. I will argue that while currently there is no justification for a formal definition containing (C2), there is reason to think that we might be able to construct an adequate theological basis and a viable philosophical model for an interpretation of (C2) that understands "Mediatrix of all graces" in a sense not clearly implied by previous Marian dogmas. Given these possible theological and philosophical results, which we shall explore carefully in this chapter, a formal definition containing (C2) may very well become justified in the fullness of time. We will see that such a formal definition would arguably have far-reaching consequences for the future of the Church.

DISAMBIGUATION: INSTRUMENTAL VERSUS DISTRIBUTIVE MEDIATRIX

We may distinguish two senses in which Mary can be considered "Mediatrix of all graces":

(1) Mary is *instrumental Mediatrix* of all graces, in that God did not become human and subsequently acquire graces for us without Mary's voluntary consent to give birth to Jesus Christ.

(2) Mary is *distributive Mediatrix* of all graces, in that after her Assumption into Heaven no graces Christ acquired for sinful humans are received by them without Mary's intercessory cooperation.[1]

The superfluity of a formal definition proclaiming Mary to be instrumental yet not distributive Mediatrix is quickly ascertained by observing that Mary's being instrumental Mediatrix is implied by the Marian dogmas and formally revealed truths that the Church already teaches. As *Theotokos* Mary gave birth to the God-Man who acquired graces for us, including our redemption. That she voluntarily consented to give birth to Jesus, and so became the "neck" through which all these graces flow, is revealed by sacred Scripture in Luke 1:38.[2] And it was only possible for Mary to become the Mother of God in virtue of her Immaculate Conception. Since there is both an adequate theological basis and sufficient philosophical comprehension for these supporting truths of the faith, there is as well for the proposition that Mary is instrumental Mediatrix. Indeed, the proposition is not sufficiently distinct from previous formal definitions or definitive teachings to warrant a formal definition

1. I have adapted these formulations from Hardon, 254–55, avoiding the metaphor of Mary as "channel of all graces" Hardon uses to describe Mary as instrumental Mediatrix. It is important to note that Mary's being distributive Mediatrix would consist in her *cooperating* in the distribution of all graces acquired by Christ and received by sinful humans, not in her *solely distributing* those graces in a manner that precludes any divine role in their distribution. I shall return to this point later in the chapter.

2. The image of Mary as the neck of all graces is attributed by Pope Pius X to St. Bernardine of Sienna in *Ad Diem Illum Laetissimum* 13.

containing it or any claim to the effect that Mary is *only* instrumental Mediatrix. At least the title "Mediatrix," understood in a purely instrumental sense, isn't misleading in the way "Co-Redemptrix" is. Nonetheless, any formal definition proclaiming Mary to be merely instrumental Mediatrix of all graces is unwarranted simply because it would be redundant.

The interesting question is whether a formal definition proclaiming Mary to be Mediatrix of all graces in the distributive sense is justified—or if not currently justified, whether there is reason to think that it might become justified at some future time. The proposition that Mary is distributive Mediatrix is not an obvious consequence of previous Marian dogmas and other elements in the deposit of faith. Although these truths don't rule out the possibility that Mary cooperates in the distribution of all graces acquired by Christ and received by us, neither do they establish the actuality that she helps distribute all these graces after her Assumption. Thus we must now resume our evaluation by determining if (C2), interpreted as the proposition that Mary is distributive Mediatrix of all graces, has an adequate theological basis and is philosophically viable.

STAGE G

Is there an adequate theological basis for the proposition that Mary is distributive Mediatrix of all graces?

As was the case with the meritorious Co-Redemptrix proposition, a number of papal encyclicals seem to assert the distributive Mediatrix proposition:

> God has committed to Mary the treasury of all good things, in order that everyone may know that through her are obtained every hope, every grace, and all salvation (Pius IX).[3]

3. *Ubi Primum* 5.

The recourse we have to Mary in prayer follows upon the office she continuously fills by the side of the throne of God as Mediatrix of Divine grace; being by worthiness and by merit most acceptable to Him, and, therefore, surpassing in power all the angels and saints in Heaven (Leo XIII).[4]

With equal truth may it be also affirmed that, by the will of God, Mary is the intermediary through whom is distributed unto us this immense treasury of mercies gathered by God, for mercy and truth were created by Jesus Christ [John 1:17]. Thus as no man goeth to the Father but by the Son, so no man goeth to Christ but by His Mother (Leo XIII).[5]

It cannot, of course, be denied that the dispensation of these treasures [all the gifts that Our Savior purchased for us by His Death and by His Blood] is the particular and peculiar right of Jesus Christ . . . Nevertheless, by this companionship in sorrow and suffering already mentioned between the Mother and the Son, it has been allowed to the august Virgin to be the most powerful mediatrix and advocate of the whole world with the Divine Son (Pius X).[6]

For this reason, every kind of grace received from the treasury of the redemption is ministered as it were through the hands of the same sorrowful Virgin (Leo XV).[7]

But we know that all things are imparted to us by God, the Greatest and Best, through the hands of the Mother of God (Pius XI).[8]

4. *Iucunda Semper Expectatione* 2.
5. *Octobri Mense* 4.
6. *Ad Diem Illum Laetissimum* 13.
7. *Inter Sodaldicia* 182.
8. *Ingravescentibus Malis* 32.

> She became our Mother also when the divine Redeemer
> offered the sacrifice of Himself; and hence by this title
> also, we are her children. She teaches us all the virtues;
> she gives us her Son and with Him all the help we need,
> for "God wished us to have all things through Mary"
> (Pius XII; quotation from St. Bernard).[9]

Finally, though omitting the qualifier "omnium gratiarum," a recent conciliar document might also be taken to support the distributive Mediatrix proposition. Vatican II teaches that "taken up into heaven, she did not lay aside this saving office, but by her manifold intercession continues to bring us the gifts of eternal salvation."[10]

Earlier we noted that, as teachings of the ordinary magisterium, papal statements asserting that Mary is meritorious Co-Redemptrix do not demand an assent of faith (*de fide*), but only a religious submission of will and intellect (*obsequium religiosum*) requiring us to take such statements seriously, to examine our consciences for any unreasonable recalcitrance to them, and to remain open-minded in our consideration of them. As such, statements of the ordinary magisterium by themselves do not provide an adequate theological basis for some proposition, though they may suggest potentially fruitful lines of inquiry. This same point applies to the papal and conciliar statements concerning the proposition that Mary is distributive Mediatrix. Even assuming that all these statements unambiguously assert that after her Assumption Mary cooperates in the distribution of all graces acquired by Christ for sinful humans and received by them, it does not follow that the distributive Mediatrix proposition has been infallibly taught, or that it should be so taught, either as a primary or a secondary object of infallibility. Hence we must dig deeper if we are to discover an adequate theological basis for this proposition.

9. *Mediator Dei* 169.
10. *Lumen gentium* 62.

In the spirit of open-mindedness required by the *obsequium religiosum* we should adopt toward the foregoing teachings of the ordinary magisterium, let us consider a possible theological basis for the distributive Mediatrix proposition. At the very least, I hope that the following reflections show how the notion of Mary as distributive Mediatrix can serve as a catalyst for clarifying a number of theological issues.

The first part of the possible theological basis for Mary as distributive Mediatrix amounts to the recognition that the title "Queen of Heaven" has been enthusiastically bestowed on her through the centuries by numerous generations of the faithful.[11] Since all these devout Christians are members of the Church, which is indefectible in matters of faith, arguably their universal understanding of Mary as Queen of Heaven is an exercise of their spiritual sense of faith, or *sensus fidei*, and thus cannot be fundamentally in error.[12] Sometimes the *sensus fidei* is identified with an individualized supernatural capacity that is bestowed upon each member of the Church at his or her baptism, leading to puzzles about why the polling data comparing the spiritual insights of practicing and non-practicing Catholics rarely distinguish between these two populations—certainly an unexpected result if all have received at baptism the same power

11. Three familiar expressions of Mary's heavenly queenship are the traditional Marian antiphons *Salve Regina*, *Ave Regina Caelorum*, and *Regina Caeli*. There are also countless paintings and sculptures portraying Mary as Queen of Heaven, as well as various sacred musical compositions praising her as such. The Church also has a feast day honoring the Queenship of Mary.

12. I follow Sullivan in distinguishing between *sensus fidei* as the faithful's God-given instinct to discern truth from error in matters of faith and *sensus fidelium* as the truths the faithful discern through their exercise of this instinct. *Consensus fidelium* then consists in those truths of the faith universally agreed upon by the whole body of the faithful. See *Magisterium* 21–23. I will say a little more about this sort of corporate comprehension below.

of spiritual discernment![13] Such puzzles can be avoided by identifying the *sensus fidei* with a genuinely collective capacity for corporate comprehension. Just as a company can correctly recognize there to be an international market for its products, so through its manifold devotional practices the Holy Church can correctly recognize Mary to be Queen of Heaven.[14] On this view, that Mary is Queen of Heaven, though not a solemnly defined dogma, is nevertheless a formally revealed truth that once was implicit in the deposit of faith and over time has been made explicit by the *sensus fidei* whereby the body of the faithful as a whole "clings without fail to the faith once delivered to the saints (cf. Jude 3), penetrates it more deeply by accurate insights, and applies it more thoroughly to life."[15]

The second part of the possible theological basis for Mary as distributive Mediatrix is the observation that, as Queen of Heaven, Mary has a supremacy and eminence in the heavenly hierarchy greater than that of any other intelligent creature except her Son seated in majesty. Leo XIII describes Mary as "surpassing in power all the angels and saints in Heaven." Indeed, the queen of a domain has a supremacy and eminence second only to the king's. What property or function does Mary, though remaining substantially the same being she was on Earth, come to possess after her Assumption in virtue of which she has a supremacy and eminence second only to that of Christ, Who is God Himself? A natural answer is that, unlike any other saint or angel, after her Assumption Mary receives the power to cooperate in the distribution to sinful humans of any and all of the graces acquired

13. See Richard R. Gaillardetz, *By What Authority? A Primer on Scripture, the Magisterium, and the Sense of the Faithful* (Collegeville: Liturgical Press, 2003) 118–19.

14. A similar *sensus fidei* of Mary as immaculately conceived and of Mary as assumed into Heaven preceded the papal definitions of the third and fourth Marian dogmas, respectively.

15. *Lumen gentium* 12.

for them by Christ. This power does not guarantee that all such graces will be distributed to human recipients, but only that no such grace is distributed without Mary's intercessory cooperation. In other words, Mary is distributive Mediatrix of all graces actually received by sinful humans. Notice that the foregoing account only explains *why* Mary is distributive Mediatrix—i.e., as the concrete manifestation of her heavenly queenship. It does not yet explain *how* she is distributive Mediatrix.[16] The latter requires a viable philosophical model of the distributive Mediatrix proposition.

The third and final part of the possible theological basis takes the form of a conditional conclusion:

(CC) If (i) it is a formally revealed truth that Mary is Queen of Heaven, and (ii) the proposition that Mary is distributive Mediatrix of all graces is required for the explanation of this truth, and (iii) a viable philosophical model can be provided of how Mary is distributive Mediatrix, then a formal definition of the proposition that Mary is distributive Mediatrix of all graces is conceptually possible.

Earlier in this section we considered the reason for condition (i); in the next section we shall consider condition (iii). For now, let us consider condition (ii).

Secondary objects of infallibility include truths which, though not themselves formally revealed, are required for the explanation or defense of formally revealed truths.[17] The gist of

16. Nor does it preclude alternative theological explanations of why Mary is distributive Mediatrix. I am only developing one possible explanation.

17. There is some question whether section 88 of the most recent Catechism of the Catholic Church teaches that not only revealed truths but also truths required for the explanation or defense of revealed truths could be defined as dogmas of faith. The section in question reads:

The Church's Magisterium exercises the authority it holds from Christ to the fullest extent when it defines dogmas, that is, when it

the argument presented in this section is that since the proposition that Mary is distributive Mediatrix of all graces acquired by Christ and received by us is required for an explanation of the formally revealed truth that Mary is Queen of Heaven, the distributive Mediatrix proposition could be legitimately defined as a secondary object of infallibility. Let us deepen our understanding of the possible theological basis by exploring some possible criticisms of it.

It might be objected that Mary's being distributive Mediatrix of all graces does not really explain why Mary is Queen of Heaven. After all, being a queen involves ruling over others; whereas distributing graces seems more like a form of servitude. One might reply that the title "Queen of Heaven" should not be interpreted in literally monarchical terms, but rather ontologically as designating a level in the hierarchy of heavenly beings ordered according to their divinely bestowed powers or functions. The power or function of helping in the distribution of any graces acquired by Christ and received by sinful humans then provides a plausible explanation for why Mary occupies

---

proposes, in a form obliging the Christian people to an irrevocable adherence of faith, truths contained in the divine Revelation or also when it proposes, in a definitive way, truths having a necessary connection with these.

The consequence that any truth required for the explanation or defense of a revealed truth could itself be defined as a dogma of faith can be avoided by adopting a narrow reading of "necessary connection," according to which proposition B has a necessary connection with propositions A (which itself may be a conjunction of separate propositions) only if B logically follows from A alone. Thus the proposition that a human rose from the dead has a necessary connection with the revealed proposition that Jesus rose from the dead; however, since a proposition utilized in the explanation or defense of a revealed truth usually doesn't logically follow from that revealed truth alone, typically the former has no necessary connection with the latter. For further discussion of this matter see Francis A. Sullivan, "The 'Secondary Object' of Infallibility." *Theological Studies* 54 (1993) 536–50.

the penultimate level in this ordering: saints and angels receive the power to help distribute some of these graces by interceding before the throne of Christ. Yet Mary intercedes in each of these cases, as well as in other cases where graces are bestowed upon sinful humans without the intercessions of saints and angels. Hence only Mary receives the power to cooperate in the distribution of *all* graces acquired by Christ and received by sinful humans, which places her higher in the heavenly hierarchy than any other being except Christ Himself. That she exercises this power to serve others is fully consonant with Jesus's teaching in Mark 9:35: "If anyone wishes to be first, he shall be the last of all and the servant of all."

Another possible objection is that the proposition that Mary is distributive Mediatrix isn't actually required to explain why Mary is Queen of Heaven, since there is an alternative and equally plausible explanation for the latter. For example, a preferable explanation might consist in the fact that Mary is the Mother of the King who is seated with the Father on His throne, and whose kingdom will have no end.[18] A difficulty with this explanation is that being a "queen mother," or mother of the reigning monarch, is conceptually and ontologically distinct from being a queen. If Prince William had become King of England while Princess Diana was still alive, then she would not thereby have become Queen of England but would only have become Queen Mother. Similarly, Mary's being the Mother of Christ the King would only explain why she is "Queen Mother of Heaven," not why she is truly the Queen of Heaven.

Perhaps Mary is Queen of Heaven, not because she is distributive Mediatrix, but because there is a spiritual marriage between her and the Holy Spirit that began when she consented to become the Mother of God by being overshadowed by the Spirit

---

18. I am indebted to an anonymous reader for pressing me on this point.

and which is perfected in Heaven.[19] In response, we must ask what is the nature of this perfect spiritual marriage, especially in light of our Lord's teaching that "At the resurrection they shall neither marry nor are given in marriage but are like the angels in Heaven"(Matt 22:30). If angels in Heaven are not married, and if after her Assumption Mary is higher than any angel, then she isn't literally married to the Holy Spirit or to anyone else in Heaven. Nor is it clear what is meant by a purely *spiritual* marriage. Perhaps the sense here is figurative: in Heaven Mary enjoys a perfect spiritual marriage with the divine because there is perfect harmony between the divine will and her will, including her willingness to help distribute to sinful humans any graces Christ acquired for them through his Passion. But then Mary's spiritual marriage does not explain why she is Queen of Heaven in terms that are different from her being distributive Mediatrix; indeed, her spiritual marriage includes her being distributive Mediatrix!

I mention these possible objections and replies, not to stymie further inquiry into whether there is an adequate theological basis for the distributive Mediatrix proposition, but to show one way such an inquiry might proceed. However, even supposing that Mary's being distributive Mediatrix explains why she is Queen of Heaven in a manner preferable to any alternative explanation, at most it follows that a formal definition of the distributive Mediatrix proposition as a secondary object of infallibility is *conceptually* possible, not that there *should* be any such definition. The reason is that a solemn definition isn't simply the result of a theological exercise. It is a deeply spiritual act that goes beyond all purely intellectual concerns. Even if all three conditions in (CC) were satisfied, the extraordinary magisterium would still need to seek through prayer the guidance of the Holy Spirit. Only in accordance with this divine guidance, I believe, would a formal definition of a dogma containing the

19. A related suggestion is that in Heaven there is a perfect spiritual marriage between Mary as Mother of the Church and Christ as its Head.

proposition that Mary is distributive Mediatrix of all graces be fully justified.

STAGE H

Is there a viable philosophical model for the proposition that Mary is distributive Mediatrix of all graces?

We seek conceptual tools which will enable us to comprehend, as far as humanly possible, how the distributive Mediatrix proposition might be true. Proponents of this proposition often draw upon the traditional Mariological notion of Mary after her Assumption as *omnipotentia supplex*, the all-powerful suppliant possessing an adventitious supernatural power derived from God which enables her to help distribute any graces acquired by Christ to the spatiotemporally scattered recipients of those graces.[20] Exactly how should we understand this adventitious supernatural power?

Certainly at her Assumption Mary doesn't become a being whose essence is to be *omnipotentia supplex*, for then she would no longer be human but instead would cease to exist and be replaced by a supernatural being who evolves from her. Perhaps her being *omnipotentia supplex* is an accidental supernatural property she acquires upon her Assumption. But then what is the nature of this accidental property, and what is it like to have it? Though there may be a viable philosophical model of Mary as *omnipotentia supplex,* supporters of a fifth Marian dogma have yet to articulate it.

It is possible that there be a number of distinct and equally viable philosophical models for interpreting a given proposition. Building upon some insights of Scholastic epistemology, I will

20. For more discussion of this notion see St. Alphonsus Maria de Ligouri, *The Glories of Mary*, Part 1, trans. Charles G. Fehrenbach, C.S.S.R. et al. (Baltimore: Helicon Press, 1962) 113.

now develop two such models of how Mary in Heaven distributes graces acquired by Christ. After briefly describing St. Thomas Aquinas's account of how angels have natural knowledge of creatures and their activities, I will explain how the supernatural knowledge Mary requires to be distributive Mediatrix might be comprehended in similar terms. I will then explore a somewhat different suggestion by Scotus of how Mary in Heaven can have all the supernatural knowledge of earthly creatures she requires in order to cooperate in the distribution to them of graces acquired by Christ.

In the view of St. Thomas, there is an act of cognition or thought whenever a form—in more modern parlance, a universal concept—exists independently of the individuating conditions of matter.[21] For example, when the concept *horse*, which my intellect has abstracted from my sensory experiences of particular horses, exists in my mind, I have a thought of horses. When I correctly apply this concept to something real to make a judgment (e.g., that Zanjero is a horse), my thought counts as an instance of genuine knowledge. Hence there is an act of knowledge whenever a universal concept not only exists independently of individuating conditions but is also correctly applied to something real. Furthermore, Aquinas maintains that an act of knowledge need not subsist in a material agent, just as heat need not subsist in fire.[22] He identifies these disembodied acts of knowledge with purely spiritual intelligences, or angels.

Since angels lack sense organs, they do not abstract universal concepts applying to natural things from experience; rather, each angel literally *is* a universal concept—more precisely, a self-knowing, independently existing species, or trope—created by God in such a way that it virtually includes an innate concept of every natural thing and its condition or activity.[23] An analogy

21. See *Summa Theologiae* 1a q.85 a.1–2.

22. See ibid., 1a q.56 a.1.

23. See ibid., 1a q.56 a.2.

may prove useful in understanding what Aquinas has in mind here. The determinable concept *triangle* virtually includes determinant concepts applying to each specific type of triangle: *scalene, isosceles, right*, etc. Similarly, an angel is an independently existing determinable concept virtually including determinant concepts of each natural thing and its condition or activity. For example, one angel might be identified with the determinable *actually possessing some degree of goodness* which virtually includes determinant concepts applying to each real being: *God, man born on such-and-such date and performing such-and-such actions* (=a determinant concept applying to Socrates), *horse with such-and-such dimensions and abilities* (=a determinant concept applying to Zanjero), etc. Other angels might be identified with distinct determinable concepts—for example, *actually ordered to some end*—which also virtually include determinant concepts applying to every real being. For Aquinas, since each angel qua immaterial determinable exists independently of matter, it is a disembodied act of cognition. And since each angel qua immaterial determinable virtually includes determinants correctly applying to, among other things, every past, present, and future human petitioning for grace, Aquinas concludes that an angel is naturally capable of knowing each and every such petitioner.[24]

Initially, it is unclear how St. Thomas's view of angelic knowledge could apply to Mary in Heaven. Mary is not a disembodied spiritual intelligence but remains a human being with a body and sense organs after her Assumption. As such, she is not

24. Although an angel is naturally capable of knowing any specific being, it need not constantly know every specific being. An angel with the potentiality of knowing every human being who has ever lived may actually know only some subset of them, so that unlike in the case of God there is some admixture of potentiality and actuality in angelic knowing. See ibid., 1a q.56 a.1. Aquinas also holds that higher angels know all natural beings through fewer, or less complex, determinable concepts (e.g., *actual*) than do lower angels (e.g., *actually ordered to some end*), so that there is an angelic hierarchy; see ibid., 1a q.55 a.3.

a universal determinable concept containing determinant concepts applying to each and every real being. However, Aquinas's discussion of the human soul's knowledge after death but before being reunited with its resurrected body provides a clue as to how Mary in Heaven might possess something similar to angelic knowledge. According to St. Thomas, disembodied human souls don't know things via sense-images. Nor do they know things through concepts acquired in life, since even the souls of infants who have died without acquiring any natural knowledge can still acquire supernatural knowledge. Rather, such souls know things by concepts supplied by God, in a way similar to how angels understand.[25] Specifically, God supplies a disembodied human soul with determinable concepts—e.g., *color*—and the power of grasping these concepts to a degree that the soul perfectly comprehends every determinant virtually included in the determinable—e.g., *scarlet*, *vermilion*, etc. Thus disembodied human souls know supernaturally what angels know naturally, though to a lesser degree.[26] In the case of Mary after her Assumption, even though she possesses a glorified body God could supply her soul with a determinable concept—e.g., *historical human petitioning for grace*—and the power of discriminating the determinants virtually included in this determinable to such a degree that Mary's soul perfectly knows each actual petitioner—e.g., *monk making his confession at such-and-such location on such-*

25. Ibid., 1a q.89 a.1.

26. The supernatural knowledge disembodied human souls possess is lesser than the natural knowledge angels because, as inferior intellectual natures, human souls receive "a greater number of species [concepts], which are less universal and bestow a lower degree of comprehension." This point is clear from the example given in the text, since unlike the universal determinable concepts/species which angels are and whereby they naturally know things (by knowing themselves), the determinable concepts whereby disembodied human souls supernaturally know things (e.g., *color*) are less extensive.

and-such date (=Thomas Merton on June 14, 1960, at the Abbey of Gethsemani), etc.[27]

One question about this Thomist model is how God bestows on Mary's soul the power to discriminate the determinants of the determinable concept to such a degree that her soul supernaturally knows any given petitioner the way an angel can naturally. Another question is whether the Thomist model does justice to why Mary occupies a place in Heaven greater than that of any other saint or angel. It cannot be by virtue of her supernaturally acquired knowledge, since St. Thomas takes the highest angels to possess such knowledge in a superior fashion—i.e., by knowing all actual things through a single universal determinable concept. Nonetheless, if no grace is received by a sinful human except through Mary's intercessory cooperation as distributive Mediatrix, then it seems that Mary must have knowledge of every past, present, and future human being petitioning for grace before she can intercede for them. Interestingly, in the Litany of Loreto Mary is addressed as "Mirror of Justice," suggesting that in Heaven she somehow functions as a reflection of her Son. Let us now try to develop this suggestion philosophically by drawing upon some ideas of Duns Scotus.

Scotus holds that God Himself has formally distinct ideas of every possible and actual creature.[28] God knows an actual crea-

27. To simplify my exposition, in this chapter I speak of potential human recipients of grace as "petitioners" for grace. However, it is possible for someone to receive grace without explicitly asking for it. The philosophical models to be developed of how Mary helps distribute to sinful humans any graces acquired by Christ are meant to include cases where Mary knows and desires that someone who condignly or congruously merits a grace without asking for it receive it. (In chapter 4, I will restrict "petitioners" to those who ask Mary to intercede on behalf of a specific intention.)

28. *Ordinatio* 2, d. 3, pars 1, q. 6. English translation by Paul Vincent Spade in *Five Texts on the Mediaeval Problem of Universals: Porphyry, Boethius, Abelard, Duns Scotus, Ockham* (Indianapolis: Hackett) 108. Entities are formally distinct if and only if there is a less-than-real

ture by knowing His formally distinct idea of it and by knowing His formally distinct act of will whereby He created the creature and conserves it in being. The totality of divine ideas is contained in the wisdom of the Word, the second Person of the Holy Trinity, Who is hypostatically united to the human body and the human soul of Jesus Christ now seated in majesty in Heaven.

The will is guided by the intellect. Therefore, in order for Mary's intercessory acts of will to cooperate in the distribution of any grace acquired by Christ, Mary must first know each and every past, present, and future sinful human petitioning for grace. Herself a human being, Mary does not possess this knowledge by natural means. On the Thomist model, she possesses it via supernaturally acquired concepts and associated powers of discrimination. Scotus's theory of divine ideas in the Word allows us to see another way she might possess such knowledge. Blessed humans in Heaven enjoy a supernatural vision of God in His glory. In the case of Mary, from among the totality of divine ideas contained in the Word, Christ seated in majesty reveals to her formally distinct ideas of each and every sinful human petitioning for grace as part of her supernatural vision.[29] Consequently, in knowing these divine ideas revealed to her by Christ, Mary knows each human petitioning for grace by what

----

difference between them (so that they can't exist independently of each other) which is nonetheless more-than-conceptual (so that the difference isn't merely in our minds). An intuitive example is a triangle's properties of being equilateral and equiangular. Scotus believes that a merely formal distinction among ideas in the divine intellect is compatible with divine simplicity. For more on the formal distinction in Duns Scotus see Peter King's "Scotus on Metaphysics" in *The Cambridge Companion to Duns Scotus* (Cambridge: Cambridge University Press, 2003) 15–68 (especially 22–25).

29. Christ might also reveal to her that the petitioners represented by these ideas have been created and are conserved by an act of divine will, perhaps by instructing her that he will reveal to her no ideas of merely possible petitioners.

Scotus calls a "quasi-reflex act," the primary object of which is the divine idea and the secondary object of which is the petitioner represented by that idea.[30]

It might be wondered how Mary's mind, even after her Assumption, is capable of having divine ideas. But properly speaking, on the Scotist model Mary does not have divine ideas in the way God does—viz., as intrinsic features of her essence. Rather, God uses His divine ideas to reveal to her earthly persons and events remote from her heavenly vicinity, just as He did in the case of certain prophets. For example, Jeremiah says of the plot against him that "I knew it because the Lord informed me; at that time you, O Lord, *showed* me their doings" (Jer 11:18, emphasis added). God showed Jeremiah the doings of plotters remote from the prophet's vicinity by revealing to Jeremiah what God already knew on the basis of His divine ideas of the plotters. Thus these divine ideas were made accessible to Jeremiah (he was not *told* but *shown*) even though they were not intrinsic features of his human essence. On the Scotist model, God does the same for Mary in Heaven regarding earthly petitioners for grace.

On the basis of her quasi-reflex acts of knowledge, Mary then exercises quasi-reflex acts of will to intercede for the petitioners presented by these same divine ideas. Because God has ordained that any grace acquired for us by Christ is not distributed to a recipient without Mary's freewill cooperation, Mary alone intercedes in this manner, in that her intercessory act is a secondary instrumental cause or occasion God uses to distribute

---

30. *Ord.* III, suppl., dist. 28. English translation by Allan B. Wolter in *Duns Scotus on the Will and Morality* (Washington D.C.: The Catholic University of America Press, 1997) 289. There Scotus applies the notion of a quasi-reflex act to the habit of charity: in loving God as perfect good, I will that others love Him too, so that in addition to my primary act directed at God there is a quasi-reflex act directed at others. I am adapting Scotus's point to Mary's knowledge in Heaven, which is primarily directed at God and His divine ideas of actual petitioners and secondarily directed at these actual petitioners themselves.

the grace. In line with 1 Cor 12:11, according to which the Holy Spirit distributes graces "to each person as He wishes," we may even say that Mary's intercessory act is a secondary instrumental cause/occasion used by the Holy Spirit as primary cause to distribute any grace acquired by Christ to a human recipient.[31] Saints and angels so intercede in some instances, but only Mary so intercedes in all. It is not her supernatural knowledge of all petitioners, which is a function of her intellect, but rather her universal loving intercession on behalf of all petitioners, which is a function of her will unique to her, that, on the Scotist model, makes Mary Queen of Heaven—though certainly her knowledge is necessary for her intercession.

On the Scotist model, Mary's quasi-reflex acts of knowledge and will occur in temporal succession, implying that in Heaven she must be subject to some kind of time. However, it does not follow that the formally distinct divine ideas Mary knows must themselves be in time, any more than a mathematician's successive acts of knowledge and will when she adds a series of numbers require that these numbers be in time. Non-temporal realities can be present to temporal beings. Nor must Mary somehow squeeze all her quasi-reflex acts of knowledge and will between her Assumption and the Final Judgment. Theoretically, Mary might continue to know divine ideas of petitioners and to intercede for them before the throne of Christ for an indefinitely long period after the Final Judgment. For example, even if John Smith receives the grace of perseverance before Mary's intercession on Smith's behalf, based on His foreknowledge of Mary's intercession—which is a foreseen congruous merit of hers—the Holy Spirit may elect to bestow this grace upon Smith. The only thing necessary, it seems, is that Mary not know whether Smith has already received this grace. For if she knew

31. Again, I am thankful to an anonymous reader for pressing me to clarify this point.

that he has already received it, her asking that he receive it would lack any motive.[32]

My purpose in presenting these two models is neither to prove that Mary is distributive Mediatrix nor to settle every outstanding question about the views of Aquinas and Scotus. It is simply to provide a tolerably clear picture of how Mary might cooperate in the distribution of all graces acquired by Christ to spatiotemporally scattered human recipients after her Assumption without compromising her essential humanity. The fact that Mary is *omnipotentia supplex* consists in nothing besides her natural ability to ask for mercy based upon certain determinable concepts supplied to her by God (the Thomist model) or upon supernatural knowledge revealed to her by the Word which she reflects (the Scotist model). Consequently, there is no temptation to treat Mary in Heaven as a quasi-divine being. Perhaps other philosopher-theologians can improve upon the models sketched here, or develop alternative models drawn from different intellectual traditions. I heartily encourage this kind of philosophical exploration. The more ways we have of understanding how Mary might act as distributive Mediatrix of all graces, the better.

We now consolidate the results of this section and the previous one. In the last section, I argued that the first two conditions of the conditional conclusion (CC) are satisfied: it is a formally revealed truth that Mary is Queen of Heaven, and the proposition that Mary is distributive Mediatrix of all graces is required for the explanation of this truth. In the current section I developed two philosophical models of how Mary is distributive Mediatrix, at least one of which—the Scotist model—I take to be viable. (With further development the Thomist model may also become viable.) Hence we have some reason to believe that the

32. For an interesting discussion of related issues, see Michael Dummett's "Bringing About the Past" in *Truth and Other Enigmas* (Cambridge: Harvard University Press, 1978) 333–50.

third condition of (CC) is also satisfied. Pending corroboration of these results, we may tentatively infer that a formal definition of the proposition that Mary is distributive Mediatrix of all graces is conceptually possible. Should the Holy Spirit provide the extraordinary magisterium with the proper guidance at some future time, a formal definition of the distributive Mediatrix proposition will become fully justified.

Possible Consequences of a Formal Definition

Let us imagine a possible future in which the pope declares the proposition that Mary is distributive Mediatrix of all graces to be a dogma of the faith, or at least a secondary object of infallibility. The members of Vox Populi Mariae Mediatrici believe that one consequence of such a formal definition would be tremendous graces flowing to the world through the Church.[33] Yet there might also be an unexpected consequence which these same members, many of whom are highly traditional Catholics, would find unpalatable.

To continue with our hypothetical scenario, imagine a future theologian in the aftermath of the formal definition who reflects that since Mary is distributive Mediatrix of *all* graces, *ipso facto* she is distributive Mediatrix of all graces bestowed during the Mass. By that time, suppose that in addition to the models developed here, several other viable models have been developed of how Mary can help distribute these graces without her being physically present at every altar during the Consecration. Armed

33. "The examples of other dogmas of the Church can be instructive in reminding us that many of the precise 'hows' have not been concluded to, but this does not stop the Church and the tremendous graces that flow to the Church and the world by solemnly defining these truths" (Miravalle, response to my comments on Episode #14 of "Co-Redemptrix, Mediatrix, Advocate," http://www.airmaria.com/?p=580#comments). I will respond to this claim in the conclusion of the current work.

with these conceptual resources, the theologian reflects further that since grace is bestowed during the Mass through the bread and wine that have been transformed into the body, soul, and divinity of Christ, as distributive Mediatrix Mary's intercessory cooperation is involved in the bestowal of even this grace.

Suddenly the theologian is struck by an intriguing train of thought: in terms of its role within the Eucharist, Mary's intercessory cooperation is metaphysically similar to that of the priest who consecrates the elements. For, with the Thomist, we may identify Mary's act of Eucharistic intercession and the priest's act of consecration as secondary instrumental causes which God as primary cause uses to transform the bread and wine into Christ's body, soul, and divinity through which grace flows to partakers of the sacrament; alternatively, with the Scotist, we may identify Mary's act of Eucharistic intercession and the priest's act of consecration not as causes but as occasions which God has ordained the bread and wine to become Christ's body, soul, and divinity through which grace flows. In either case, Mary seems to be acting as a priest. And if Mary, who is a woman, acts as a priest, then it is unclear why other women cannot be ordained to the priesthood.

The theologian publishes his reflections and receives a number of skeptical responses. Some readers object that "Christ alone truly offered the sacrifice of atonement on the Cross. Mary gave him moral support in this action. She is therefore not entitled to the name 'priest,' as several Roman documents legislate."[34] The theologian replies that if not truly offering the sacrifice of atonement on the Cross disqualifies Mary from being a priest, then it also disqualifies anyone besides Christ from being a priest, since no one else literally died on the Cross for our sins. Other readers object that "the Lord Jesus chose men (*viri*) to form the college of the twelve apostles, and the apostles did the same when they chose collaborators to succeed them in

34. Hardon, 255.

their ministry . . . For this reason the ordination of women is not possible."[35] While agreeing that Christ chose only men to form the apostolic college, the theologian observes that Christ also chose Mary to be distributive Mediatrix, so that all "priestly graces"—specifically, those graces which are bestowed through the sacrifice of the Mass, absolution from sin during Confession, sanctification, and so forth—are given partly on the basis of Mary's freewill cooperation. If the Lord Jesus's choice of male apostles legitimizes admitting men to the priesthood, the theologian asks, then why doesn't our Lord's choice of his Mother to be distributive Mediatrix of all graces, including priestly ones, legitimize admitting women to the priesthood as well?

A subtler objection is that the apostles and their priestly successors receive a consecrating power which, when exercised under the proper ritualistic conditions, guarantees that the bread and wine are transformed into the body, soul, and divinity of Christ. By contrast, Mary's intercession on behalf of a petitioner does not guarantee that the petitioner will receive the grace he or she requests. In reply, the theologian allows that not every grace requested by a petitioner is bestowed upon him or her with the aid of Mary's intercession.[36] However, there is no doubt that the priestly graces are bestowed on rightly disposed recipients as long as the proper ritualistic conditions are satisfied. Specifically, there is no doubt that during the Eucharist the bread and wine are transformed into Christ's body, soul, and divinity so that the redemptive grace Christ acquired through his Passion, as well as other graces he acquired, are distributed to rightly disposed partakers of this sacrament.[37] If Mary really cooperates in the

35. *Catechism of the Catholic Church* sec. 1577.

36. In the next chapter, as part of our evaluation of the claim that Mary is Advocate, we shall consider the consequences of Mary's intercession when certain graces are requested yet not bestowed.

37. These additional graces Christ acquired through his Passion include spiritual nourishment, the forgiveness of venial sins, and the

distribution of *any* grace, including the graces associated with the Eucharist, then her act of Eucharistic intercession is not just a concomitant to the distribution of these graces. No less than the celebrant's consecrating act, her intercessory act plays a part in the actual distribution of these graces—either as a contributing instrumental cause or as a contributing occasion.[38] Without insisting on radical reforms, the theologian cautiously concludes that the truth of the distributive Mediatrix proposition makes it appreciably more difficult to defend an exclusively male clergy.

As more theologians join what has become a vigorous and healthy debate, a popular movement emerges in support of a papal definition permitting the ordination of women as priests. Polls are taken and petitions are circulated calling upon the Holy Father to act decisively in favor of a genuinely Marian priesthood. Taking notice of these developments, members of the doctrinally conservative episcopate begin to weigh in on the matter. Many of the bishops worry that using the distributive Mediatrix doctrine as a basis for ordaining women as priests would contravene the Church's traditional teaching that only men can be priests—at the very least something non-infallibly taught by the ordinary magisterium and thus demanding *obsequium religiosum*, possibly something even taught definitively by

---

strength to attain eternal glory (*vitaticum*). As Aquinas observes, "by this sacrament we are made partakers of our Lord's Passion" (*Summa Theologiae* 3 q.83 a.1). As distributive Mediatrix of all graces, Mary in Heaven plays an integral role in the distribution of these sacramental graces through her acts of Eucharistic intercession.

38. Given that partaking of Christ's body, soul, and divinity in the Eucharist under the appropriate conditions and right interior dispositions (e.g., without being conscious of mortal sin) immediately bestows these graces upon the recipient, both Mary's intercessory act and the celebrant's consecrating act are contributing instrumental causes or contributing occasions of the transubstantiation. There is no other point at which Mary's intercessory act might operate in the distribution of Eucharistic graces.

the ordinary universal magisterium as a primary object of infallibility and thus demanding *de fide* assent. The bishops warn that for the Church to admit women priests now would be for the Church to admit that it was wrong in refusing to admit women priests before.

Respecting these deep concerns, our hypothetical theologian responds with a carefully worded letter to the bishops. He concedes that the Congregation for the Doctrine of the Faith has declared that the doctrine that women cannot be ordained to the priesthood has been infallibly taught by the ordinary universal magisterium. Yet what is the nature of this "cannot?" Presumably it is within God's absolute power to endow earthly women with the same power to help distribute priestly graces with which only earthly men have hitherto been endowed; denying this possibility shortchanges divine omnipotence. Even so, there may be another sense in which woman cannot be priests so long as the ordinary universal magisterium infallibly teaches that they cannot.

The theologian then asks the bishops to suppose that a king chooses ministers to assist him in governing the kingdom. The king invests this "ministerium" with the power of laying down definitive criteria for selecting subsequent ministers. The power of the ministerium is infallible because the king ordains that, for all time, only whoever satisfies the criteria stipulated by the ministerium is eligible to become a minister. The ministerium decides that only men over fifty can become ministers; women cannot. Nonetheless, the infallibility of this ministerial power is perfectly compatible with the ministerium broadening its criteria at some future time. Suppose that two thousand years later, certain considerations lead the ministerium to stipulate that women over fifty can also become ministers. The later stipulation does not contradict the earlier one. Instead, at different points in its history the ministerium exercises in diverse ways one and the same infallible power of determining the criteria for becoming a minister. In neither case has the ministerium made a mistake.

Similarly, our theologian argues, Christ has invested the teaching office of his Church with the infallible power of exercising its prudent judgment to determine, among other things, who can serve as a member of the clergy. The fact that the magisterium has prudently elected to exercise this power one way up to now is fully compatible with the magisterium prudently electing to exercise it differently at some point in the future. There are at least two kinds of infallibility: reflective and refractive. Reflective infallibility mirrors those holy truths which never change, such as that Mary was conceived free of Original Sin and was assumed bodily into Heaven. Refractive infallibility receives a divinely bestowed authority and selectively applies or "bends" it one way or the other to determine aspects of our Christian life together. For various reasons, up to the present the magisterium has prudently elected to exercise its refractive infallible power to allow only men to become priests. The culture into which the Church was born was gripped by a rabid patriarchy that continued into the Middle Ages and beyond. Permitting women priests might have raised such a scandal that the nascent Christian religion would have been smothered in its crib. Moreover, the importance of re-interpreting many pagan ceremonies from a Christian perspective while maintaining a sharp distinction between Christianity and pagan religions, many of which featured priestesses, may very well have contributed to the Church's decision to restrict the priesthood to men. Once these reasons are no longer operative, without contradicting itself it is possible for the magisterium to ease this restriction through the prudent exercise of one and the same refractive infallible power. Of course, the magisterium should do so when and only when it is moved by the Holy Spirit—or so our hypothetical theologian proposes.

Understandably, these speculations might seem flimsy and far-fetched. Is there really any authority for the distinction between reflective and refractive infallibility? To see why there is, let us apply to the current issue Scotus's insights concerning the possibility of dispensations from some of the Commandments. These insights rise above mere theory mongering because they are deeply attuned to Scriptural realities.[39]

The problem Scotus addresses is the apparent contradiction between the status of the Commandments as precepts of natural law, which are necessary truths, and Biblical cases in which God apparently dispensed certain holy persons from these precepts. For example, how can the fifth Commandment prohibiting the killing of innocents be a necessary moral law if Abraham was commanded to sacrifice his son Isaac?[40] Scotus replies that only the first two Commandments are necessary truths strictly pertaining to the natural law: based on an understanding of what "God" means, natural reason can discern that one and only one supremely lovable God must exist; and if God is supremely lovable, then it follows that nothing else should be worshiped as God, nor must He be shown any irreverence by taking His name in vain. According to Scotus, Commandments four through ten are not necessary truths, and thus do not pertain to the law of nature in the strict sense.[41] Nevertheless, they pertain to the natural law in an extended sense because, though not necessary, they are "exceedingly in harmony" with the first two Commandments. To explain what he means, Scotus uses the analogy of civic peace and private property. That we ought to seek peace in society is a necessary moral law. Yet it does not logically follow that there should be a law permitting people to own private property, since peace is logically possible in a society allowing only common

39. Scotus's discussion is found in *Ordinatio* 3, suppl., dist. 37. In Wolter, 198–207.

40. Other examples Scotus mentions are God's permitting the departing Israelites to steal from or despoil the Egyptians and commanding the prophet Hosea to marry a harlot and fornicate with her to have children.

41. Scotus remains uncertain about the status of the Third Commandment prescribing observance of the Sabbath.

property. Nevertheless, permitting people to have their own possessions is an extremely good way of facilitating civic peace, and so a law instituting private property is exceedingly in harmony with the law of peace. In the same way, Commandments four through ten facilitate love and honor of God, even though they are not logically implied by the first two Commandments.[42]

A similar Scotist point can be made about the priesthood. Ordaining only male priests has been exceedingly in harmony with the law of nature, since for centuries doing so has promoted love and honor of the one true God through the rituals of the Church. However, strictly speaking it is not a necessary truth that only men should be ordained as priests. For it is logically possible not only that a woman be endowed with priestly powers but also that in exercising these powers she promotes love and honor of God. Indeed, if Mary is distributive Mediatrix of all graces, including the priestly ones, then it is not only a logically possibility but an actuality that a woman has promoted love and honor of God through the exercise of the priestly powers with which she has been endowed. Thus the possibility exists of a future dispensation from the earlier restriction of the priesthood to men.

A logical possibility, or even a single actual instance, is one thing; instituting a new precept is quite another. How might a dispensation permitting women priests *in general* be motivated? Here Scotus's account of the rationale for dispensing from a non-necessary precept of the natural law is germane.[43] Scotus considers the case of marriage, the primary purpose of which he takes to be the procreation of children who are raised in the faith, and a secondary purpose of which he takes to be avoidance of fornication. Scotus argues that when a thing has both a pri-

42. Scotus gives the example of the blessed in Heaven, who love and honor God without caring for their old and infirm parents in accordance with the Fourth Commandment. For in Heaven there is no old age or infirmity.

43. See *Ordinatio* 4, dist. 33, q.1. In Wolter, 208–12.

mary and a secondary purpose, it is reasonable to use the thing in a manner that favors the primary purpose, even if doing so sometimes militates against the secondary purpose. In extreme circumstances, as when Christianity is threatened with extinction because too many children have been killed in a war or plague, fulfilling the primary purpose of marriage would make it prudent to dispense from the moral precept of monogamy, and bigamy would be morally licit—indeed, morally imperative to ensure the survival of the Church.

A related case, our hypothetical theologian might argue, is when the primary purpose of something can be fulfilled without contravening its secondary purpose because the latter is simply no longer operative. The primary purpose of the priesthood is promoting love and honor of God through the sacraments; a secondary purpose is avoiding scandal that would destroy the Church. In the early ages of Christianity, the primary purpose of the priesthood could only be fulfilled by avoiding deadly scandal posed by allowing female priests, which in turn made it prudent to ordain only male priests. In present times, however, broad cultural changes have made the threat of deadly scandal posed by allowing women priests no longer operative. Therefore, prudently bending the criteria to allow women priests would not contradict the earlier restriction, any more than prudently dispensing from the law of monogamy under certain circumstances to allow bigamy would contradict the earlier law. As Scotus says, "All that would be wanting for complete justice would be divine approbation, which perhaps would then occur and be revealed in a special way to the Church."[44] If such approbation were forthcoming, the magisterium's decision to broaden the criteria for the priesthood to include women would then become a certain moral precept no less infallible in its circumstances than the

44. Ibid. Thus I disagree with a hyper-rationalist reading of Scotus, according to which the rationale for dispensation can be discerned solely by the use of right reason. Right revelation is also required.

earlier decision was in its circumstances. In other words, each decision is an act of what has been called refractive infallibility.[45]

~

Only time will tell whether something like the possible future I have sketched will become actual. Summarizing the results of this chapter, a formal definition of a dogma containing (C2), interpreted as the proposition that Mary is distributive Mediatrix of all graces, is not currently justified. Yet since there is reason to think that this proposition has an adequate theological basis and a viable philosophical model, there is also reason to think that a formal definition of this proposition as a secondary object of infallibility will become justified. At such time, the Church may very well find itself facing the prospect of a fundamental change which is nevertheless deeply consonant with the infallible power of its teaching authority.

45. Though a full analysis of the nature of infallibility lies beyond the scope of this essay, the account presented here is not committed to a maximalist interpretation of papal infallibility, according to which the pope alone can issue infallible declarations without input from the episcopate. For it is consistent with what has been said that an exercise of refractive infallibility by the ordinary and universal magisterium—for example, a dispensation allowing women priests—is an essentially *collective* act that the pope and bishops must perform in unity and unison under the guidance of the Holy Spirit.

CHAPTER 4

Mary as Advocate:
The Guarantee of Divine Aid

THE FINAL claim contained in the proposed fifth Marian dogma is

(C3) Mary is Advocate because she acts as our principle intercessor before Christ.

In light of the fact that for centuries the faithful have asked Mary to intercede for them more frequently than they have requested the intercession of any other venerable, blessed, saint, or angel in the history of the Church, (C3) appears patently obvious. On the other hand, we will see that the different senses in which Mary may be supposed to act as our principle intercessor can easily lead to confusion. Furthermore, the understanding of Mary's Advocacy encouraged by traditional devotional practices seems to face an intractable problem. To avoid all confusion and to address this problem, it might be thought that a formal definition of a dogma containing the proper interpretation of (C3) is needed. The focus of the current chapter is whether such a formal definition is necessary, or whether what has already been formally revealed is sufficient to answer any questions that arise about Marian Advocacy.

DISAMBIGUATION

Universal versus non-universal Advocate,
partially versus fully efficacious Advocate,
addressed versus non-addressed Advocate

Capitalization of "Advocate" suggests that Mary is unique in performing whatever function this title designates. To hone in on Mary's *sui generis* form of Advocacy, it will help to draw several distinctions which can then tested against both our religious experience and what is revealed by sacred tradition.

We restrict our attention to situations in which a person is in real need of a specific grace, whether or nor the person asks for it, and where there is no impediment in the person to receiving the grace in question (as when someone in need of baptism is conscious of being in a state of mortal sin). Call such a person a *potential recipient* of the specific grace. The first distinction concerns the scope of Mary's Advocacy:

(1) Mary is *universal Advocate*, in that she intercedes for any potential recipient by asking that he/she receive the needed grace.

(2) Mary is *non-universal Advocate*, in that there are some potential recipients for whom she intercedes by asking that they receive the needed graces and other potential recipients for whom she does not intercede by asking that they receive the needed graces.[1]

Is there any reason to prefer one characterization over the other?

1. Strictly speaking, there is a potential recipient for whom Mary intercedes and a recipient for whom she does not intercede. (This statement could apply to the same potential recipient on different occasions, or to distinct potential recipients.) We set aside the merely logical possibility that there are potential recipients but that Mary doesn't intercede for any of them, since however we understand Marian Advocacy it is a formally revealed truth of the Catholic faith that Mary intercedes for at least some people by supporting their prayers for graces they need.

First and foremost, Mary is a mother in the fullest sense. Thus whenever she intercedes on behalf of a potential recipient, her act is fundamentally maternal: she sees that the person needs a specific grace and she immediately desires that the person receive this grace, just as a mother who sees her children in need of food immediately desires that they receive food. It is difficult to understand how Mary's Advocacy could be truly maternal if she desired that only some of those who need certain graces receive them, any more than it is understandable how a genuine mother could desire that only some of her children who need food receive it. Therefore, there is strong reason to prefer a characterization of Mary, who is the ultimate Mother, as universal rather than non-universal Advocate.[2]

Let it be granted, then, that Mary intercedes for any potential recipient by asking that he/she receive the needed grace. The next distinction concerns the effectiveness of Mary's Advocacy:

(3) Mary is *fully efficacious Advocate*, in that whenever she intercedes for a potential recipient, he/she receives the needed grace.

(4) Mary is *partially efficacious Advocate*, in that some potential recipients for whom she intercedes receive the needed grace and other potential recipient for whom she intercedes does not receive the needed grace.[3]

2. There is a connection here with a Christology of universal atonement: just Christ died to offer the possibility of redemption to everyone, not just to some as the Calvinist doctrine of "limited atonement" would have it, so Mary intercedes on behalf of all who need grace, not just on behalf of some in a sort of "limited intercession."

3. Strictly speaking, there is a potential recipient for whom Mary intercedes who receives the needed grace and a potential recipient for whom she intercedes who does not receive the needed grace (as before, either the same potential recipient on different occasions, or distinct potential recipients.) Because we believe on faith that at least some of the potential recipients for whom Mary intercedes receive the graces they need, we set aside the merely logical possibility that there are

Again, we ask whether there is any reason to prefer one characterization over the other.

So far we have concentrated on the graces associated with baptism, redemption, sanctification, and glorification. Some of these graces, such as eternal glory, can be condignly merited by someone in a state of sanctity, so that God's fidelity to His promises guarantees that the needed grace is bestowed upon the recipient. However, a grace is any divine gift, including common graces such as food desired by someone hungry or clothing desired by someone naked. In many cases there is no any impediment in the person to receiving a common grace he/she needs. A virtuous father might ask Mary to pray that his virtuous daughter receive the common grace of being healed from the bone cancer afflicting her. From our religious experience, we know many instances where a potential recipient in need of some grace does not receive it. The hungry person starves, the naked person freezes, and virtuous daughter succumbs to her terminal illness. Since Mary is universal Advocate, she intercedes for each of these potential recipients by asking that they receive the needed graces. Yet these potential recipients do not receive the specific graces of food, clothing, and healing. God may withhold the requested graces and instead turn the sufferings of these potential recipients to comparable or even greater good in the fullness of time through the mystery of His Providence. Thus it is undeniable there are some potential recipients for whom Mary intercedes by asking that they receive certain graces they need without these recipients receiving these graces. Our religious experience seems to bear out the fact that, at best, Mary is partially efficacious Advocate. In the next two sections, we shall determine if any more can be said about the efficacy of her Advocacy.

A third distinction concerns whether or not someone asks Mary to intercede on behalf of a potential recipient:

---

potential recipients for each one of whom Mary intercedes without any one of them receiving the needed grace.

(5) Mary is *addressed Advocate* whenever someone prays that she intercede for a potential recipient by asking that he/she receive the needed grace (including cases where the petitioner and the potential recipient are the same).

(6) Mary is *non-addressed Advocate* whenever she intercedes for a potential recipient by asking that he/she receive the needed grace without someone praying that she intercede in such a manner.

Given that Mary is a mother in the fullest sense, it is highly likely that she often acts as non-addressed Advocate, just as an ordinary mother desires that her children receive the food they need even if they don't ask for it. And we know that innumerable times in the history of the Church people have prayed to Mary that she intercede on behalf on their intentions for the bestowal of specific graces. Hence in some cases she is addressed, whereas in others she is non-addressed, Advocate.

Finally, let a *remembered potential recipient* be one for whom someone has prayed to Mary that she intercede on the potential recipient's behalf by asking that he/she receive the needed grace. Factoring the third into the second distinction, we may say that:

(7) Mary is *fully efficacious addressed Advocate* if and only if whenever Mary intercedes for a remembered potential recipient, he/she receives the needed grace; otherwise, Mary is *partially efficacious addressed Advocate.*

Actual cases like that of the virtuous father and his virtuous daughter suffering from bone cancer seem to bear out that, at best, Mary is partially efficacious addressed Advocate.

With these distinctions in place, we now wish to learn what sacred tradition teaches concerning the nature of Mary's Advocacy. To do so, we must complete our overall evaluation of the proposed fifth Marian dogma.

STAGE I

Is there an adequate theological basis for the proposition that Mary is Advocate in some suitable sense?

We saw that Mary is addressed as Queen of Heaven in traditional prayers, such as *Salve Regina*. In the same prayer, Mary is also addressed as Advocate:

> Hail, holy Queen, Mother of mercy;
> Hail our life, our sweetness, and our hope.
> To you do we cry, poor banished children of Eve.
> To you do we send up our sighs,
> Mourning and weeping in this valley of tears.
> Turn then, most gracious Advocate,
> your eyes of mercy toward us;
> And after this our exile, show unto us
> The blessed fruit of your womb, Jesus.
> O clement, O loving, O sweet Virgin Mary!
> Pray for us, O Holy Mother of God,
> That we may be made worthy of the promises of Christ.
> Amen.

Another traditional prayer, the *Memorare*, sometimes mistakenly attributed to St. Bernard of Clairvaux but actually based on a longer 15th-century prayer and later popularized by Fr. Claude Bernard (1588–1641), has something to say about the nature of Mary's Advocacy:

> Remember, O most gracious Virgin Mary,
> That never was it known that anyone
> who fled to your protection,
> Implored your help, or sought your intercession,
> was left unaided.
> Inspired by this confidence,
> I fly unto you, O Virgin of Virgins, my Mother.
> To you do I come, before you I stand,
> sinful and sorrowful.

O Mother of the Word Incarnate,
Despise not my petitions, but in your mercy
hear and answer me.
Amen.

According to the first three lines, anyone who asks Mary to intercede is guaranteed to receive divine aid. Taken together, these traditional prayers seem to present a formally revealed understanding of the Blessed Mother in Heaven as a gracious, firmly reliable Advocate whose intercession is always granted. Apparently, then, there is an adequate theological basis for the proposition that Mary is Advocate in some suitable sense, and accordingly for (C3).

However, as described in the last section, our religious experience conflicts with this confident assessment. Sometimes, even when Mary intercedes for a remembered potential recipient by asking that the specific grace he/she needs be bestowed, the needed grace is not forthcoming. The virtuous father asks Mary to pray that his virtuous daughter be healed of bone cancer; he may even recite the *Salve Regina* or the *Memorare*, and still his daughter does not receive the grace of healing. As we saw, at most Mary is partially efficacious addressed Advocate. Yet the *Memorare* seems to depict Mary as fully efficacious addressed Advocate. Rather than recovering an adequate theological basis for (C3), haven't we have uncovered a contradiction between sacred tradition and religious experience?

On the other hand, perhaps the contradiction is only apparent. Philosophical reflection might suggest a logically possible manner of reconciling Mary's fully efficacious Advocacy when interceding for a remembered potential recipient with the fact that the specific grace she asks to be bestowed upon a remembered potential recipient is sometimes not bestowed. But even supposing such a logically possibility, it remains wholly abstract unless theological reflection provides it with concrete content. By cooperating along these lines, philosophy and theology might establish both an adequate theological basis and a viable philosophical model for the proposition that Mary is Advocate in a suitable sense. Let us see whether these two disciplines can cooperate to find a single solution.

STAGE J

Is there a viable philosophical model for the proposition that Mary is Advocate in some suitable sense?

The philosophical models we developed of how Mary could cooperate in the distributing all graces also explain how she could act as universal addressed or non-addressed Advocate. On the Thomist model, her soul receives from God a determinable concept containing determinant concepts of each and every potential recipient, remembered or otherwise, for whom she then intercedes. On the Scotist model, her quasi-reflex acts of knowledge—whose primary objects are the divine ideas of potential recipients revealed to her by the Word and whose secondary objects are the potential recipients represented by these ideas—serve as the basis for her quasi-reflex acts of will whereby she desires that each potential recipient receive the grace he/she needs. When these graces are bestowed, God uses Mary's quasi-reflex intercessory acts as secondary causes or occasions to distribute the needed graces; otherwise, Mary advocates the bestowal of these graces without actually distributing them. We now seek a philosophical model of Advocacy that goes beyond these models by explaining how Mary can be, as the *Memorare* implies, an absolutely reliable addressed Advocate, even when sometimes the specific requested graces are not bestowed on a remembered potential recipient.

A careful inspection of the first three lines of the *Memorare* offers a clue: "Remember, O most gracious Virgin Mary, that never was it known that anyone who fled to your protection, implored your help, or sought your intercession, was left unaided."

This fact inspires the confidence that anyone seeking Mary's intercession is guaranteed to receive aid, not from humanity, but from God. However, there is no guarantee that the specific grace requested by the petitioner will be bestowed, but only that the petitioner will receive *some* form of divine aid. For example, the *Memorare* does not guarantee that when the virtuous father asks Mary to intercede on behalf of his daughter, the child will receive the grace of healing he asks to be bestowed on her. There is only the guarantee that he (and, given that his prayer is a truly self-less act intended to benefit his daughter, the child herself) will receive divine aid which may or may not consist in that specific grace. Modifying our third distinction, we may then say that:

(9) Mary is *guaranteed efficacious addressed Advocate* if and only if whenever she intercedes for a remembered potential recipient, he/she receives some grace that may or may not be the requested one.

Philosophically, the possibility that Mary is guaranteed effica-cious addressed Advocate, as the *Memorare* teaches, is per-fectly compatible with her being partially efficacious addressed Advocate, as we learn from religious experience. Asking Mary to intercede on behalf of a specific intention does not guarantee that the intention will be granted. It only guarantees that divine aid will be.

Questions remain. We have already noted that for any grace—requested or otherwise—to be bestowed on a potential recipient, there must be no impediment in him/her to receiving that grace. For there to be a guarantee of divine aid, must the petitioner who asks Mary to intercede on behalf of the remem-bered potential recipient also satisfy certain conditions? For example, must he not be conscious of mortal sin, and must he also possess the right interior disposition? Moreover, the forego-ing philosophical account is highly abstract. If in many cases the divine aid bestowed on the remembered potential recipient is other than the requested grace, then what is the nature of this aid? Can we say anything more definite about it?

In *Raccolta*, a book listing prayers and other acts of devotion to which popes have attached indulgences, Pope Pius IX declared that a partial indulgence is earned by anyone who recites the *Memorare* with contrition; and that a plenary indulgence is earned by anyone who recites it once a month, makes sacramental Confession, receives sacramental Communion, and also visits a church or chapel to pray for the intentions of the Holy Father.[4] The Church teaches that when a person sins, even once the sin is forgiven a temporal punishment is owed to make perfect satisfaction. Such satisfaction is usually provided by a deceased person's soul during its existence in Purgatory. Earned indulgences may be applied to remit a person's temporal debt: either part of the debt is remitted, as in a partial indulgence; or the entire debt is remitted, as in a plenary indulgence.[5]

The first observation to make is that proper recitation of the *Memorare* is a sacramental. Sacramentals stand midway between ordinary good works and the sacraments. Like an ordinary good work, the power of a sacramental to confer grace depends primarily on the interior disposition of the person who performs it (*ex opere operantis*). For example, reciting the *Memorare* earns a partial indulgence only if it is done with contrition. By contrast, the power of a sacrament to confer grace depends primarily on the proper ritualistic acts being performed (*ex opere operato*). For example, regardless of his interior disposition, a priest who performs the Eucharistic rite makes Christ's body, blood, and divinity available to communicants. Yet like a sacrament, a sacramental is tied to a particular object, such as holy water sprinkled

---

4. *Raccolta* 92 (1846). Available online at http://members.aol.com/liturgialatina/raccolta/mary.htm.

5. Needless to say, any buying, selling, or bartering of indulgences bespeaks an unholy cynicism that is strictly incompatible with the spirit of sincere piety necessary for the conferral of these graces.

on the congregation, or a particular devotion, such as reciting the *Memorare* once a month. Using these objects or performing these devotions with the right interior disposition ensures that grace is conferred.

A second observation is that, according to the *Memorare*'s opening lines, *no one* who has ever sought Mary's intercession has been left unaided. The petitioner hopes that by doing what these others have done, he/she too will receive divine aid. And what the petitioner does includes standing "sinful and sorrowful" before the Mother of the Word Incarnate. The clear implication is that whoever in a spirit of contrition asks Mary to intercede—whether in the exact words of the *Memorare* or not—will receive divine aid, either as grace conferred upon the petitioner or upon the one for whom the petitioner prays. Hence the *Memorare* designates all these prayers as secondary sacramentals: even though their words may vary, as long as they are addressed to Mary with the right interior disposition of contrition, the conferral of grace is guaranteed.

The last observation pertains to the nature of the graces conferred by contrite acts of prayer requesting Mary's intercession on behalf of some intention. We can use our earlier example of the father asking Mary to pray for his sick daughter to receive the grace of healing, even though she does not receive it, as a prism to refract a broad spectrum of possibilities. At one end of the spectrum is a situation where the father recites the *Memorare* while satisfying the conditions for bestowal of a plenary indulgence. Provided there is no impediment in the daughter, such as consciousness of mortal sin, though she isn't healed the entire temporal debt incurred by her sins is remitted. If the father merely recites the *Memorare* with contrition, or if in any manner whatsoever he contritely asks Mary to intercede on his daughter's behalf in any manner whatsoever, then at least part of the temporal debt incurred by his daughter's sins is remitted. At other end of the spectrum is a situation where a hungry person humbly asks Mary for food and instead receives either the strength to go on looking for food or, should he perish before finding it, partial remission of the temporal debt incurred by his sins.

Interesting situations between these extremes include ones in which the father satisfies the conditions for bestowal of either a plenary or a partial indulgence and the daughter has, unbeknownst to him, already remitted the entire temporal debt incurred by her sins through an act of penance. By hypothesis she does not receive the grace of healing, and by supposition she has no temporal debt to be remitted. How, then, does she receive divine aid through Mary's intercession? She might still receive graces needed for her to attain eternal glory. Or the graces earned by proper recitation of the *Memorare* or other Marian prayers may redound to the father, in the form of profound comfort in the knowledge that his daughter is no longer suffering and lives with God forever. Graces may even redound to another sick child in a manner that helps the original father and daughter more deeply understand in the fullness of time God's loving Providence for all His creatures. The point is not to put our Lord and our Lady into a box by nailing down their precise ministrations to those who pray for those in need, which we can never do, but rather to give a sense of the wide arena in which these ministrations operate.

Through a long tradition of sacramentals such as the *Memorare* and other Marian prayers, the *sensus fidei* reveals an understanding of Mary as a totally reliable Advocate. This understanding is something contained in the deposit of faith that has become clearer to the faithful over the centuries. Through the exercise of natural reason, philosophy reveals a logical possibility that reconciles the traditional understanding of Mary's Advocacy with the admitted fact that sometimes the graces she prays to be bestowed are not bestowed—namely, the possibility that her intercession acts as a secondary cause/occasion of the bestowal of some grace other than the requested one. Finally, through Pius IX's theological clarification of the efficacy of Mary's

Advocacy in his gloss on the *Memorare* and, by extension, other Marian prayers, the purely abstract logical possibility is injected with precise content: anyone who contritely seeks Mary's intercession can rest assured that some good will come of it—if not the specifically requested grace, then other graces which remit temporal debts incurred by sin or bestow other benefits. Among all the angels and saints, only Mary enjoys this privilege. We conclude that there is both an adequate theological basis and a viable philosophical model for (C3) interpreted as the proposition that Mary is (guaranteed efficacious addressed) Advocate.

STAGE K

Is the proposition that Mary is (guaranteed efficacious addressed) Advocate sufficiently distinct from previous formal definitions or definitive teachings?

From what we have said in the present chapter, the answer is plainly no. All the materials sufficient to derive a theological basis and a philosophical model for (C3) interpreted in the aforementioned sense are explicit and time-honored elements in the deposit of faith. Even though Pius IX's declaration of the indulgences earned by proper recitation of the *Memorare* is a teaching of the ordinary magisterium, the renewed confidence with which subsequent generations of the faithful contritely recite the *Memorare* and other Marian prayers as sacramentals shows how the declaration makes explicitly known what was implicitly understood all along. Consequently, the papal definition of a dogma containing (C3) interpreted as the proposition that Mary is guaranteed efficacious addressed Advocate would be nothing but a redundancy, a mere stutter of what has already been definitely taught.

Conclusion

A Plea for Marian Moderation

IT IS tempting to view contemporary Mariology as a protracted battle between minimalists and maximalists. Minimalists wish to prevent the formal definition of any Marian dogma ascribing to Mary a role other than giving Christ a body free from the penalties due to Original Sin. More bluntly, the minimalists try to come as close as possible to a high Protestant understanding of Mary without being Protestants. On the other hand, maximalists wish for the formal definition of a Marian dogma proclaiming her instrumental and meritorious Co-Redemptrix, instrumental and distributive Mediatrix of all graces, and supreme Advocate. Less charitably, the maximalists try to come as close as possible to making Mary divine without being guilty of Mariolatry. I believe that the dichotomy between minimalism and maximalism has unhelpfully polarized Mariology by offering either-or alternatives which tend to stifle rather than stimulate progress in the field.

In this book I have tried to reclaim the middle ground. The moderate position developed in these pages is not a grayish blurring of the extremes but, hopefully, a powerful third alternative that draws upon minimalist and maximalist insights while charting a course that is respectful of tradition yet open to principled change. I expect stiff resistance on both flanks, particularly from Marian maximalists. To anticipate some of this resistance, as well as to focus the moderate approach I favor, I conclude with a polemic against ten reasons Dr. Mark Miravalle gives for the formal definition of a fifth Marian dogma.[1]

1. Dr. Miravalle presents these reasons in the June 18, June 21, and

83

REASON #1

The formal definition of Mary as Co-Redemptrix, Mediatrix of all graces, and Advocate will add theological clarity to teachings containing these terms.

Reply: If some term is unclear, then formally defining as a dogma a teaching containing the term doesn't ensure clarity by itself. To take a simple example from the history of philosophy, the obscurity of the term "analytic" is hardly rectified merely by declaring that the teaching according to which some sentences are analytic is an irrevocable truth. Similarly, simply declaring Mary to be Co-Redemptrix, Mediatrix of all graces, and Advocate does not suffice to bring theological clarity to these terms, which we have seen are somewhat unclear. For genuine clarification to occur, disambiguation, theological motivation, and philosophical interpretation are also needed. If these intellectual components are missing, then any formal definition will have the untoward affect of requiring the faithful to believe something they don't understand.

REASON #2

The formal definition of a fifth Marian dogma would have untold ecumenical benefits.

Reply: Admittedly, in the aftermath of Pope Pius XII's declaration of the dogma of the Assumption in 1950, there was resurgence of ecumenism in the Second Vatican Council and beyond. Such a correlation may lead proponents of a fifth Marian dogma to hope for a similar resurgence in the aftermath of a formal defini-

---

June 23 (2008) episodes of "Marycast," which are archived at the following link: http://66.84.28.204/category/air-maria-shows/marycast/page/4/. Since the archive is frequently updated, readers may need to search it for the dates of these particular episodes. The archive may be searched by clicking on either the "Previous Entries" or the "Next Entries" button at the top of the page.

tion declaring Mary as Co-Redemptrix, Mediatrix of all graces, and Advocate.

However, even if the later ecumenical resurgence was largely a consequence of the earlier definition, and not just something that followed it, adequate theological and philosophical development existed for the doctrine of the Assumption before it was declared a dogma. The doctrine has its theological basis in the prior dogma of the Immaculate Conception, since Mary's preservative redemption also preserved her from all consequences of sin, including death and bodily corruption. Philosophically, the omnipotent power Christ exercised to ascend into Heaven was also exercised by him to assume his sinless Mother into Heaven. Though not fully comprehensible to human reason, neither is this divine power repugnant to it. The burden of the present work has been to show that much of the proposed fifth Marian dogma lacks comparable theological and philosophical development. Thus from the premise that a properly developed dogma has promoted ecumenism, we should not infer that a dogma that has not been properly developed will do the same.

Sadly, the renewed ecumenism of recent years has not led to a mending of the divisions between Catholic and non-Catholic Christians. Hence even supposing that the proposed fifth Marian dogma were developed to the same degree as the dogmas of the Immaculate Conception and the Assumption, there is no reason to believe that a fifth dogma will lead to an ecumenism culminating in the true Christian unity of one Church. A prerequisite for such unity may be the availability of a scale of epistemic stances toward some theological proposition, coupled with a willingness to acknowledge that others whose stance toward that particular proposition is lower on the scale than mine are nonetheless members in good standing of the same Church that I am. For example, am I willing to acknowledge someone as a Catholic who regards the proposition that Mary was immaculately conceived as more than logically possible yet less than absolutely certain?

No formal definition alone can provide answers to this and related questions; only hard and humble work can.

REASON #3

The proposed definition will affirm the dignity of the human person, particularly the dignity of woman.

Reply: Declaring Mary to be the Mother of God (*Theotokos*), as does the first Marian dogma, already affirms the fundamental dignity of woman to the fullest extent possible. For there is no possible way for a human being to be more dignified than by giving birth to the hypostatic union of the Word with a human soul and a human body in the person of Jesus Christ. Furthermore, since Mary's Divine Motherhood required her fiat or consent, the same dogma affirms the dignity of woman's cooperation with Gods' plan. Woman's ongoing dignity in this life is affirmed by the dogma of Mary's Perpetual Virginity; and the dignity of woman's elevation to eternal glory in Heaven is affirmed by the dogma of the Mary's Assumption. What other dignity of woman is left to be affirmed by the proposed fifth Marian dogma?

It might be argued that the dignity of woman's ongoing cooperation with God even in Heaven and her special meritorious cooperation with Christ in his work of ordinary redemption remain to be affirmed. Regarding the first dignity, in chapter 4 we saw that Mary's post-Assumption role as guaranteed efficacious addressed Advocate is already an explicit element of the deposit of faith requiring no formal definition. Thus even if a formal definition proclaiming Mary to be distributive Mediatrix might someday be justified, as we suggested in chapter 3, this envisaged formal definition is not necessary to affirm the dignity of woman's heavenly cooperation with God. Regarding the second dignity, in chapter 2 we saw that Mary's alleged role as meritorious Co-Redemptrix cannot be justified theologically and philosophically. Therefore, there is no such dignity of woman that a formal definition might affirm.

REASON #4

The proposed definition will serve as a corrective to the contemporary misunderstanding of woman's dignity.

Reply: The proposed definition can serve as a corrective to a misunderstanding of woman's dignity only if it can affirm woman's true dignity in a way that has not already been affirmed. From the immediately previous reply, clearly the latter is not the case. Any corrective should instead consist in reaffirming and deepening our comprehension of previous Marian dogmas.

Moreover, if the proposed definition proclaims Mary to be distributive Mediatrix of *all* graces, including the priestly ones, then it could very well serve as a corrective to the widespread misunderstanding of woman's dignity, not just in contemporary culture but also in the contemporary Church. For, as was suggested in chapter 3, acceptance of the distributive Mediatrix proposition may lead the Church to rethink its current opposition to the ordination of women to the priesthood. Rather than restoring some older, more traditional version of Catholicism, definition of a dogma containing this proposition might reap the unexpected consequence of Marian female priests in a new Church that nevertheless remains true to Her ancient roots.

REASON #5

The proposed definition will be a reaffirmation of the need for human cooperation in salvation.

Reply: The envisaged reaffirmation is intended as a response to extreme predestinationist views, according to which the exercise of human freedom in no way cooperates with divine grace in the work of ordinary redemption. However, previous Marian dogmas and formally revealed truths of sacred Scripture and tradition place ample emphasis on the exercise of Mary's freedom through her non-meritorious cooperation with God in the work of human redemption: her consenting to become the Mother of God, her raising Christ in holiness and assisting him in his adult ministry, and her consenting to his suffering and death on the Cross. Frankly, it is difficult to fathom how the need for human freewill cooperation in salvation can be stressed more strongly than by combining the foregoing illustrations from the life of Mary with Catholic teaching about the importance of human freedom in preserving sanctity, such as contritely seeking mercy through the sacrament of Confession when sanctity is lost through mortal sin. It might be argued that these examples of non-meritorious cooperation in the work of salvation so far have not eliminated extreme "*sola fide*" accounts of salvation; and that only by attributing to Mary some meritorious cooperation with Christ in the work of ordinary redemption will such views be definitely refuted. Yet any such refutation is mere fantasy until proponents of a fifth Marian dogma have solved the problems confronting the notion that Mary is meritorious Co-Redemptrix, described in chapter 2. No formal definition by itself will solve them.

REASON #6

The proposed definition will streamline for the Church the truth that suffering is redemptive.

Reply: Suffering can certainly be redemptive. Christ's suffering on Calvary redeemed Mary by preserving her from ever contracting Original Sin and redeemed other humans by freeing them from it, provided that they become and remain members of the body of Christ. Through prayer, possibly combined with suffering, Mary herself or even an ordinary person in a state of sanctity can congruously merit for an unbaptized person the application of redemptive grace whereby the recipient is exempted from the penalties due to Original Sin. The truth that suffering is redemptive is already streamlined for the Church in the substance of the faith She professes and Her ingrained theological understanding of it. Therefore, to communicate succinctly the redemptive value of suffering, there is no need to attribute to Mary the function of co-meriting with Christ our salvation, as the proposed fifth dogma would do. On the contrary, the meritorious Co-Redemptrix proposition threatens to confound the Church with unsound ideas.

REASON #7

Teaching the full truth about Mary, as does the proposed definition, will deliver a gift of unity within the Church by filling in the gaps in our understanding of her.

Reply: I agree that teaching the full truth about Mary can promote internal unity through shared comprehension *(consensus fidelium)*. But teaching the full truth about Mary also involves clarifying what she is *not*. Theoretically, explaining why Mary is not meritorious Co-Redemptrix and why certain accounts of how she might function as distributive Mediatrix make no sense could result in a basic Mariological comprehension shared by the faithful that is just as conducive to unity in the Church as the definition of a fifth Marian dogma would be. Since either the negative clarification or the positive definition could have these results, the promise of fuller Marian comprehension and greater Church unity is no reason to prefer the definition to the clarification.

REASON #8

Numerous saints through the ages, including more recent ones like Bl. Josemaría Escrivá, Bl. Padre Pio, Bl. Edith Stein, Bl. Sister Lucia of Fatima, and Bl. Mother Theresa, refer to Mary as Co-Redemptrix, Mediatrix of all graces, and Advocate.

Reply: Because these references do not address the ambiguities surrounding the terms "Co-Redemptrix," "Mediatrix," and "Advocate," they do not reflect a precise and uniform understanding of what it is for Mary to be Co-Redemptrix, Mediatrix of all Graces, and Advocate—any more than do the scattered references to Mary as "Co-Redemptrix" and "Mediatrix" in various papal encyclicals and addresses. Hence these saints' remarks do not provide a rationale for the definition of a dogma in which the constituent claims that Mary is Co-Redemptrix, Mediatrix of all graces, and Advocate are given precise theological and philosophical content.

Does the fact that saints have referred to Mary in these ways mean that we must give an assent of faith, or at least a very high degree of *obsequium religiosum*, to the belief that the constituent claims have an as-yet-undiscovered precise theological and philosophical content that Roman Catholics have a duty to discover? No. As persons who eventually become canonized, saints are certainly members of the Church whose remarks regarding matters of faith should be taken very seriously. Yet unless a saint is also a pope or a bishop, the saint is not part of the ordinary magisterium. Thus as a rule remarks made by saints regarding matters of faith do not demand even the degree of *obsequium religiosum* applicable to teachings of the ordinary magisterium, let alone an assent of faith. The wisdom of saints contributes to the *sensus fidei*—perhaps preeminently—and it demands our respect. Yet no matter how preeminent they are, individual contributions to this collective capacity for discerning truths of the faith are hardly infallible.

REASON #9

The proposed definition will lead to the fulfillment of the Fatima prophecy, "In the end my Immaculate Heart will triumph."

Reply: Prophecies derive much of their power from their enigmatic character. Like parables, they capture listeners' attention through forceful and compressed language that conveys a core meaning whose implications are nonetheless subject to a variety of interpretations.

Proponents of a fifth Marian dogma interpret the Fatima prophecies as implying that a papal definition of Mary as Co-Redemptrix, Mediatrix of all graces, and Advocate will be the "key" that unlocks Mary's heart, allowing new graces to flow to the Church and the world. Yet strictly speaking, at Fatima our Lady prophesies only that her Immaculate Heart will triumph, without specifying the precise manner in which the triumph will occur. It might occur through the envisaged papal definition—or it might occur in some other way. Proponents of a fifth dogma rightly claim that God does not force grace upon us without our freewill cooperation, and they see a dogmatic definition as the form our freewill cooperation must take to release the graces our Lady promised at Fatima. But surely another way these same graces could be released is simply by more and more people contritely asking Mary to intercede for the good of the Church and the world. Given Mary's role as guaranteed efficacious addressed Advocate discussed in chapter 4, the certain result of such widespread devotion would be many goods flowing to the Church and the world (even if not necessarily all the ones specifically requested by petitioners) without any formal definition of a fifth Marian dogma.

Lastly, although the Church has deemed the apparitions at Fatima worthy of belief, as private revelations outside the public revelation of the Catholic faith essentially completed by the end of Apostolic times, the Fatima prophecies demand neither an assent of faith nor the high degree of *obsequium religiosum* associated with secondary objects of infallibility. Therefore, as with some saints' references to Mary as "Co-Redemptrix," etc., even if the Fatima prophecies unambiguously decreed Mary to be Co-Redemptrix, Mediatrix of all graces, and Advocate, Roman Catholics would not be obliged, on pain of apostasy, to believe that these claims have an as-yet-undiscovered theological and philosophical content justifying the formal definition of a dogma containing them.[2]

REASON #10

The proposed formal definition will encourage Mary's intercession for graces to help mitigate moral degeneration, natural disaster, and total war.

Reply: Given Mary's universal Advocacy, we know that she is already interceding for these common graces. Maybe a papal definition of the proposed fifth Marian dogma will contribute to these graces flowing to the world. Maybe it won't. Since we are ultimately ignorant of the workings of divine Providence, so far we have no reason to think that these graces are not already flowing to the world in the absence of a papal definition, or that they will eventually flow to the world regardless of whether or not there is any such definition. Again, we should avoid putting our Lady and our Lord into a box of our own design and instead

2. The same point applies to the messages Ida Peerdeman allegedly received from the Blessed Virgin Mary under the title "Lady of all Nations" between 1945 and 1955, to which some Catholics appeal in support of the proposed fifth Marian dogma.

keep our hearts and minds open to the multitude of unexpected ways He may bestow graces through her intercession.

∼

I have completed my evaluation of the proposed fifth Marian dogma proclaiming that (C1) Mary is Co-Redemptrix because she cooperates preeminently with Christ in the work of redemption; that (C2) Mary is Mediatrix of all graces because she mediates any and all graces merited by Christ which are bestowed upon us; and that (C3) Mary is Advocate because she acts as our principle intercessor before Christ. Having now disambiguated each claim and considered whether it has an adequate theological basis and a viable philosophical interpretation, I conclude that a formal definition of the proposed dogma is not currently justified and is unlikely to be justified at any future time. For a formal definition including (C1) is unlikely ever to be justified; and a formal definition including (C3) is unnecessary because its legitimate content is already an explicit element of the deposit of faith. Though a formal definition including (C2) is not currently justified, I argued that it may become justified in the fullness of time, with potentially far-reaching consequences for the Church.

If the views defended here are wrong, then I pray that my presentation of them will stimulate others to learn and convey the truth about Mary so far as is humanly possible. I also pray for the Holy Father and the bishops as they reflect on these difficult questions. Most of all, I pray that my efforts will honor our Lady and glorify our Lord. *Soli Deo Gloria*.